Flipping Good!

SUDI PIGOTT

PHOTOGRAPHY BY MAJA SMEND

KYLE BOOKS

TO MY TOTALLY INCREDIBLE AND STILL PANCAKE-LOVING SON THEO

First published in Great Britain in 2017 by
Kyle Books, an imprint of Kyle Cathie Ltd
192–198 Vauxhall Bridge Road, London, SW1V 1DX
general.enquiries@kylebooks.com
www.kylebooks.co.uk

10 9 8 7 6 5 4 3 2 1

ISBN 978 0 85783 411 9

Editor: Judith Hannam
Editorial Assistant: Hannah Coughlin
Copy Editor: Jan Cutler
Designer: Nicky Collings
Photographer: Maja Smend
Illustrator: Ohn Mar Win
Food Stylist: Lizzie Harris
Prop Stylist: Tonia Shuttleworth
Production: Nic Jones and Gemma John

A Cataloguing in Publication record for this title is available
from the British Library.

Colour reproduction by f1 colour.
Printed and bound in China by 1010 Printing International Ltd

Contents

Introduction

Who says pancakes should only be eaten with lemon and sugar? There is a world beyond for the gastronomically curious. Pancakes in all their delicious diversity have long been one of the most pleasurable, life-affirming parts of my culinary explorations, from the crisp outside, chewy within *cong you bing* I first discovered in Singapore, to chestnut flour *necci* in Tuscany. My friends call me 'the pancake doyenne' as I always return from holidays relishing new recipes to expand my repertoire. But it's not just me: pancakes arouse equally enthusiastic feelings in others. I'd go as far as to say it's a truth universally consumed – we all love pancakes. They make us happy and the everyday special, and the ritual in the preparing, cooking and flipping merely adds to their appeal. They can be both a quintessential comfort food and a decadent, intimate, even elegant treat. Most are easy to rustle up using a few, usually inexpensive, and infinitely versatile, savoury or sweet ingredients, plus they're speedy to make, even if their perfection requires a little prowess. A few take longer, but that's usually resting time and the results are so rewarding.

Pancakes are much loved as portable street food around the world. I treasure memories of my regular fix of creamy garlic mushroom-filled crêpes cooked to order at a stall on Hampstead High Street after a long stroll on the Heath close to my first flat in London. I recall waiting hungrily in line as the sound of the crêpe sizzling as it hit the pan made me drool in anticipation. Among my other favourites are the steaming hot, crunchy *socca* found in Nice. I also adore ground maize Columbian *arepas* and turmeric-laden paper-thin rice flour and coconut milk Vietnamese *banh xeo* stuffed with crunchy vegetables. Almost every global culture has its pancake, and *Flipping Good!* contains recipes from more than 25 countries, from as-thin-as-one-dares French crêpes to lacy fermented South Indian dosa and exotically fragrant Arabic *atayef.*

What's more, pancakes are often associated with celebration and festival. Long before Shrove Tuesday, the final feast day when all good things have to be consumed before the start of Lent, pancakes were made to mark the end of winter and the beginning of spring. According to the pagan festival of Maslenitsa, the changes of the season were a struggle between Jarilo, the god of vegetation, fertility and spring, and the evil spirits of cold, darkness and winter. It was believed that to help vanquish winter and bring in spring, hot, round pancakes symbolising the sun should be eaten to bring its warmth and power. In France, *la Chandeleur*, or Candlemas, is celebrated on 2 February, and eating crêpes – usually filled with apple or cherries – is said to bring a year of happiness. Throughout Scandinavia, *æbleskiver*, distinctive puffy, spherical pancakes cooked in a special cast-iron pan with little hollows, are particularly associated with Christmas-morning breakfast. For the Jewish celebration of lights – Hannukah – grated potato pancakes, latkes, are enjoyed with huge relish.

Pancakes are probably one of our earliest foods, dating back to prehistoric times when plant grains were ground into flour, mixed with water and cooked on a flat stone over burning embers. Grinding tools dating back more than 30,000 years have been found which suggests pancakes were popular even among Stone Age humans. We probably have the Romans to thank for the invention of the pancake as known today. One of the first recipes for a sweet batter cooked over a griddle, dating back to the fourth century, is accredited to Apicus, the legendary Roman gourmet, and consists of egg, milk and water, beaten with a little flour, fried and served with pepper and honey. Many pancake recipes from around the globe use gluten-free flours: from quinoa to coconut, and are not exclusively grains – think chestnut and chickpea

– and these are important to living and eating more cleanly, sustainably and securely with regard to both our body and planet.

Strictly speaking, a pancake is starch based and poured as a batter onto a hot surface to be cooked free form or in a mould. Although proverbially flat, when made with the right ingredients – baking powder, bicarbonate of soda, yeast, beaten egg white or carbonated water – they may rise and be supremely fluffy. The fluffiest in this book are German pancakes known as 'Dutch babies' ('Dutch' in this instance meaning 'Deutsch'), and Finnish *pannukakku*, both of which are baked in the oven. I've taken some latitude and included a number of closely related potato-based pancakes, too, from Persian *kuku* and Irish boxty to supremely light and delectable baked-potato pancakes.

PANCAKE-MAKING PROWESS
Although making pancakes of all sorts of persuasions is relatively quick and easy, there's plenty to consider in making near-perfect pancakes that are not too dense, nor unevenly cooked, nor flat when they're meant to be gloriously fluffy and, frankly, irresistible. Here are my tips on what to consider.

INGREDIENTS AND WEIGHING
Use good quality, unbleached preferably organic flour and consider ancient grains such as spelt and einkorn. For crêpes, 00 or pasta flour really does give incredibly light results. Non-gluten flour and baking powder can be substituted throughout. Eggs should be free-range, organic and large. They have bigger, more flavourful yolks that cook and taste better. I always use unsalted butter unless otherwise specified. Unrefined sugar is far better and I often substitute coconut sugar. Unwaxed lemons make a difference too. Always weigh ingredients to make sure the ratios are correct. Guesswork isn't good enough for pancakes.

HOW TO WHISK
For British pancakes and French crêpes, it is fine to whisk the batter with an electric whisk. For US-style pancakes, *dorayaki* and where a fluffy pancake is imperative, be very wary of over-mixing. Instead, whisk by hand until the wet ingredients are just incorporated into the dry ingredients and fold in egg whites with a metal spoon or spatula. Don't worry about banishing the batter of all its lumps.

RESTING
Where recipes recommend that you rest the batter, it really does make a difference, however impatient you're inclined to be. The pancakes will be distinctly more even in texture because the starch has had more time to absorb the liquid, and the air bubbles will have risen and dispersed.

USING THE CORRECT PAN
I manage extremely well with a good non-stick frying pan with a low lip to make for better flipping. With stainless steel pans, opt for either a shallow-lipped crêpe pan or omelette pan with sides curving bowl-like into the base. These are far longer lasting and should be seasoned before first use, as should sturdy and reliable cast-iron pans. To season, pour a thin layer of vegetable oil into the pan, add 2 tablespoons of table salt, heat until smoking (the salt will blacken), then turn off the heat. Armed

with oven gloves and a good wodge of kitchen paper, scour the inside purposefully. Leave to cool and wipe out again with more kitchen paper. Ideally, these pans should not be washed up, just wiped with kitchen paper. For a more thorough clean, use hot water and a scourer, but not washing up liquid, and then re-season. Their natural non-stick qualities should improve with age. The recipes for *æbelskiver*, *poffertjes* and hoppers require specialist pans, but all are widely and inexpensively available online or at ethnic shops. Americans are very fond of electric griddles for cooking pancakes, which are useful if regularly cooking for large numbers. They give good, even results, although I think they take away some of the romance of making pancakes. Pancakes can be made on an Aga too.

HEATING AND GREASING THE PAN

Temperature is key. The pan should be shimmering hot, so that a few drops of water flipped on the surface bounce and skitter before evaporating. Be sure, however, that it is not so hot as to scorch the pancakes. Start medium–high and adjust. Whether using oil or butter, use sparingly. It is imperative that it heats evenly, otherwise the pancakes are likely to burn in some areas and undercook in others.
I recommend using kitchen paper to smear the pan or, better still, a silicon or heatproof pastry brush, but be sure to wipe off any excess. Use either unsalted butter, which has a lower whey content and burns less easily, or a mixture of butter and oil, which is also less likely to burn. Ideally, clarify the butter first by melting it in a small pan. When bubbling, skim off the foamy milk proteins that rises to the surface and pour the clarified butter beneath into a small bowl.

MOVING THE PANCAKE AND FLIPPING

Don't be tempted to move the pancake too soon, although using a palette knife to check the underside is acceptable. A good indicator is that the edges of the pancake are slightly dry and don't form crumbs on the palette knife. One of the very best checks is to wait for bubbles to not only form but also to burst in the centre. Only flip once, as repeated flipping will cause pancakes to deflate or turn rubbery.

FLIPPING TECHNIQUE

The best way to flip is to hold the pan handle firmly with two hands and to jerk it upwards and slightly forwards with a sharp movement. As the pancake takes off, pull the pan back to catch it. It's a knack worth practising to wow guests. Pancakes can, however, be flipped with a palette knife too.

KEEPING PANCAKES WARM

Ideally, pancakes should be eaten immediately. The best way to keep flat pancakes or crêpes warm is to layer them up between sheets of greaseproof paper and place in a low 100°C/gas mark ¼ oven for 5–10 minutes maximum. For other pancakes, set them out in a single layer on a wire rack within a baking tray and keep them warm in a similarly low oven.

FREEZING PANCAKES

Pancakes can be frozen. Place a sheet of baking parchment between each pancake and stack them together. Wrap the pancakes tightly in foil or put them inside a heavy-duty freezer bag and freeze. Use frozen pancakes within 1 month for the best results. Defrost and re-heat in the oven.

Breakfast & Brunch

Scottish Oat Pancakes

WITH SKYR, RASPBERRIES AND THYME HONEY

This is porridge in the form of a pancake – so it's comforting, like a warm tummy hug. These pancakes, with their subtle, toasty taste, make a perfect start for breakfast or brunch, or as a dessert. Porridge oats are simply whizzed in a food processor to make a fine flour. Besides porridge, this oat pancake gets me thinking about Scottish cranachan, so I've paired it with skyr – the Icelandic yogurt that is similar to Greek yogurt with a rich, creamy texture – raspberries and thyme honey. The oat pancakes would work equally well as a savoury breakfast dish, especially as a 'full Scottish' with bacon, black pudding (haggis, if you fancy it), roasted tomato, thyme-butter sautéed mushrooms and a poached egg.

PREP 10 mins

COOK 10 mins

TOTAL 20 mins

150g porridge oats
150g self-raising flour
½ teaspoon ground cinnamon
2 large eggs, separated
400g milk, or soya or almond milk
50g butter, melted

250g tub skyr
1 large punnet raspberries
6 tablespoons thyme honey

DIETARY

USE GLUTEN-FREE
SELF-RAISING FLOUR

MAKES

12–16 x 12CM,
SERVES 4

Preheat the oven to 100°C/gas mark ¼ and warm a plate to keep the pancakes warm while you make them. Blitz the porridge oats in a food processor to make a flour.

Mix the blitzed porridge oats, flour and cinnamon together in a bowl. Whisk in the egg yolks and the milk. Put the egg whites in a clean bowl and whisk until they form soft peaks. Gently fold the whites into the batter. The batter will be fairly thick, like double cream.

Heat a heavy non-stick frying pan over a high heat. Reduce to medium–high and use a heatproof pastry brush to brush with butter. Pour in a ladleful of batter and cook for 1–2 minutes until it puffs up. Flip over and cook for 2 minutes or until lightly golden. Keep the pancakes warm and repeat with the remaining batter, adding more butter to the pan as necessary. Serve the pancakes with a scoop of skyr, a scattering of raspberries and a good drizzle of thyme honey.

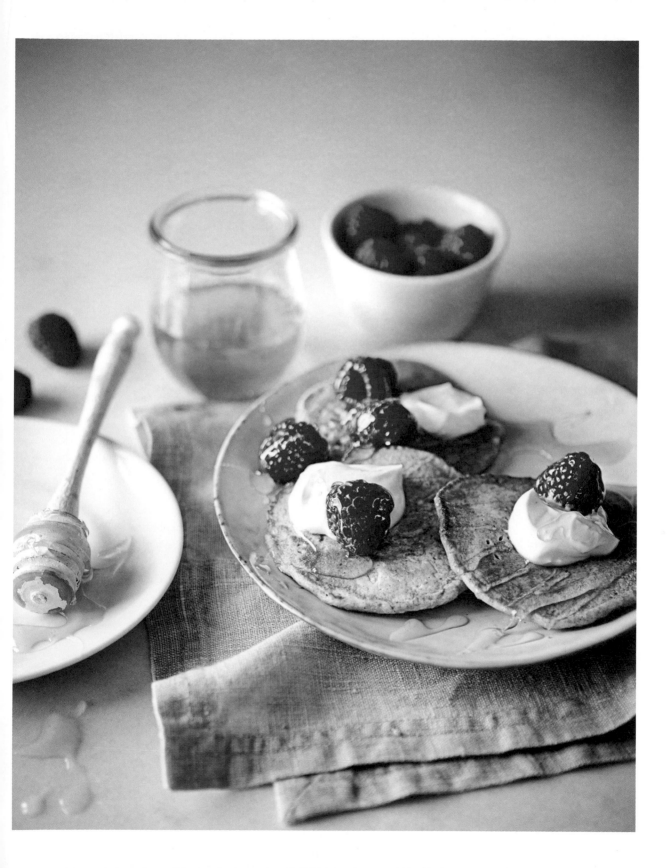

Fluffy Ricotta Pancakes

WITH RASPBERRIES AND HONEYCOMB, LIME AND GINGER BUTTER

Like sublime fluffy clouds, the texture of these pancakes is ridiculously light and delicate. Australian king of breakfast, Bill Granger, first introduced me to them even before he opened Granger & Co in London. I was blown away. They're very different from most pancakes, as they get their exceptionally light texture from the combination of ricotta and whipped egg white. Really, they are more like soufflé hotcakes than pancakes in both looks and taste. They are ideal for breakfast (they're not too messy for breakfast in bed!), and they're superb as a dessert, too, with infinite accompaniments. I also like to serve them with tangy baked rhubarb, orange and fresh ginger compote. For Aussie authenticity, I have simply pimped Bill Granger's classic honeycomb butter with lime and fresh ginger.

PREP 20 mins
*plus up to
1 hour chilling*

COOK 20 mins

TOTAL 40 mins

DIETARY

USE GLUTEN-FREE
FLOUR

MAKES

20 x 10CM,
SERVES 4–6

250g tub of ricotta, strained
2 large eggs, separated
100g plain flour, sifted
1 teaspoon baking powder
salt
zest of 2 limes
125g semi-skimmed milk
4 tablespoons coconut oil
250g raspberries, or 2 bananas, sliced

FOR THE HONEYCOMB BUTTER
150g unsalted butter, at room
temperature
zest of 1 lime
1 tablespoon lime juice
3cm piece of fresh ginger, peeled and
finely grated
75g fresh honeycomb

To make the honeycomb butter, cream the butter until soft, then add lime zest and juice, and the ginger. Gradually beat in the honeycomb. Shape into a long roll, then wrap in clingfilm and put in the freezer for 15 minutes or in the fridge for 1 hour to firm up.

Put the ricotta and egg yolks in a large bowl and mix together. Add the flour, baking powder, and a pinch of salt, then add the lime zest and milk and whisk to make a smooth batter.

Beat the egg white until foamy using a hand whisk, then gently fold into the ricotta mixture taking care not to knock the lightness out of the egg. (The mixture will keep overnight in the fridge at this stage.)

Heat a frying pan or griddle over a medium heat and add 1 tablespoon coconut oil. Drop in two large heaped dessertspoonfuls of batter and flatten to a circle, then add batter for a couple more pancakes. Cook for 1–2 minutes until they begin to bubble and turn lightly golden. Flip over and cook for 1–2 minutes until lightly golden, taking care not to let them burn.

Put the pancakes on a plate and cover with a tent of foil; this is preferable to putting them in the oven as they are so delicate that they would dry out. Repeat with the remaining batter, adding more coconut oil to the pan as before. Serve them warm with generous slices of the honeycomb butter and fresh raspberries (or sliced banana when raspberries are not in season).

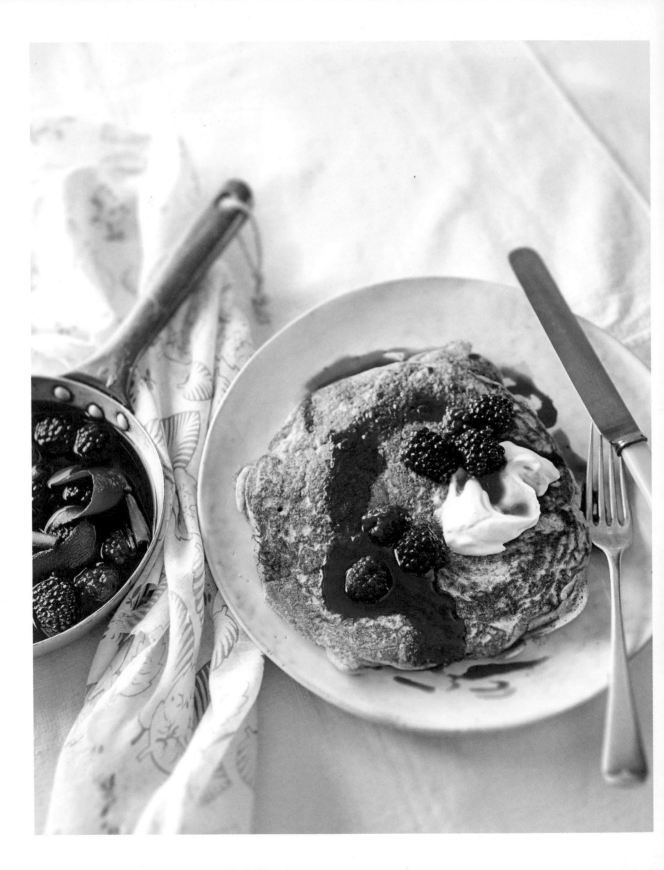

Spiced Spelt Pancake Stack

WITH CLOUDY APPLE POACHED BLACKBERRIES

The comforting flavour of the cinnamon, cardamom and nutmeg spice mix conjures up *hygge*, a very distinctive sense of cosiness that the Danes like to cultivate. Spelt flour gives a moreish nuttiness to the pancakes, and buttermilk adds a little sourness. Try sprouted spelt flour, too, for extra flavour and goodness. The pancakes won't firm up as much as non-buttermilk pancakes, so take care that they are sufficiently set before flipping them. They are perfectly good with maple syrup alone, although they go extraordinarily well with this modish, fragrant blackberry and apple sauce. Grilled bacon would make a good accompaniment for breakfast too.

PREP 10 mins

* plus 30 mins resting

COOK 35 mins

TOTAL 45 mins

DIETARY

SPELT FLOUR IS GLUTEN-FREE

MAKES

8 x 12CM, SERVES 4

250g spelt flour, sifted
1½ teaspoons baking powder
pinch of salt
2 tablespoons golden caster sugar
2 teaspoons freshly grated nutmeg
1 teaspoon cardamom seeds, crushed
2 teaspoons ground cinnamon
50g butter, melted
450ml buttermilk, plus extra if needed
1 large egg
melted butter, for cooking

FOR THE POACHED BLACKBERRIES

500ml cloudy apple juice
strips of zest from 1 orange
1 cinnamon stick
3 star anise
3 cloves
2 tablespoons wildflower honey
300g blackberries
300ml crème fraîche

Put the flour in a bowl, add the baking powder, salt and sugar, then stir in the spices and then the butter. Whisk together the buttermilk and egg, then add slowly to the batter mixture using a metal spoon. (Don't be surprised if the batter remains a little lumpy. It should take 2–3 seconds to drop from the spoon. If it is too thick, add more buttermilk; too liquid, add more flour.) Cover and rest in the fridge for at least 30 minutes, or make it the night before.

Preheat the oven to 100°C/gas mark ¼ and put a baking tray with a wire rack inside in the oven for keeping the pancakes warm while you make them. Meanwhile, to make the poached blackberries, put the apple juice in a pan over a medium–low heat and add the orange zest, cinnamon stick, star anise and cloves. Gently heat to infuse, then add the honey. Add the blackberries and gently warm through, but don't overcook, as the fruit should remain whole. Remove from the heat.

Heat a large non-stick frying pan over a medium heat and use a heatproof pastry brush to brush with butter. When the butter starts to foam, add 2 ladlefuls of batter to make a pancake, tip the pan to ensure the batter is evenly distributed in the pan, then cook for 1½ minutes or until almost set, bubbles start to form and pop on the surface and the underneath is golden. Flip over and cook for 1½ minutes or until lightly golden. Transfer to the wire rack in the oven. Repeat with the remaining batter, adding more butter to the pan as necessary. Serve with the poached blackberries and a dollop of crème fraîche.

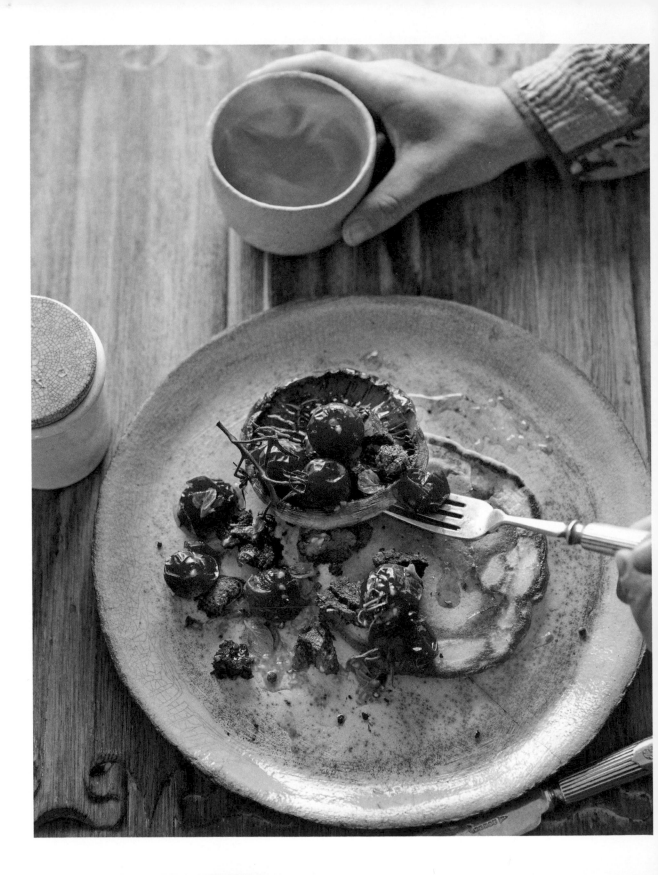

Scotch Pancakes

WITH BABY TOMATOES, MUSHROOMS AND BLACK PUDDING

I remember being obsessed with Scotch pancakes from a packet when I was young and often having them with jam as a treat when I came in from school. Nowadays I prefer them savoury with a little Parmesan, as a nod to the many Italians who settled in Scotland in the nineteenth century. For an excellent breakfast to set oneself up for a day walking in the Scottish Highlands or as a reward at the end of a good morning's ramble anywhere, combine with roasted tomatoes, grilled field mushrooms and black pudding too, if you're a fan. For an even more substantial breakfast, add some scrambled eggs with chives too. For a sweet version, omit the Parmesan and herbs, and add 2 tablespoons of golden caster sugar and a dash of vanilla extract. Serve simply with jam or fruit.

PREP 10 mins

COOK 20 mins

TOTAL 30 mins

DIETARY

USE GLUTEN-FREE FLOUR

MAKES

12 x 10CM, SERVES 4

125g self-raising flour

2 generous tablespoons grated Parmesan

1 tablespoon chopped oregano leaves

1 large egg, beaten

150ml semi-skimmed milk

3 tablespoons sunflower or rapeseed oil

salt and freshly ground black pepper

FOR THE GRILL

400g cherry tomatoes

2 tablespoons extra virgin olive oil

1 teaspoon chopped oregano leaves

400g field mushrooms, cleaned and stalks trimmed

200g black pudding, sliced

mustard, to serve

Preheat the oven to 180°C/gas mark 4. Put the tomatoes for the grill in a roasting tin, drizzle over 1 tablespoon of the oil and scatter with the oregano. Roast for 15 minutes, then reduce to 100°C/gas mark ¼ and put a plate in the oven keep the pancakes warm as you make them.

Meanwhile, sift the flour into a large bowl. Mix in the Parmesan, a pinch of salt and the oregano. Add the egg and the milk, and incorporate with an electric or hand whisk. The batter will be thick and creamy. There is no need to leave this to stand.

Heat a large, heavy frying pan over a medium heat and add 1 tablespoon sunflower oil. Spread evenly with kitchen paper. Pour in 3 dessert spoonfuls of the batter and use the tip of the spoon to form an even circle about 10cm in diameter. Add the batter for one or two more pancakes if it will fit. Cook for 2 minutes until almost set, bubbles start to form and pop on the surface and the underneath is golden. Flip over with a spatula and cook for 1–2 minutes until golden. Stack on the warmed plate whilst cooking the rest of the batter, or better still keep warm in the oven on a baking tray. Use a little more oil for each batch.

Preheat the grill or a griddle. Season the mushrooms with salt and pepper, then drizzle with the remaining olive oil. Place, stalk-side up, on the grill rack or griddle. Cook for 1–2 minutes, then turn them over and cook for 3–4 minutes until golden. Don't move the mushrooms around too much while cooking, as this releases the natural juices and makes them soggy.

At the same time, grill or griddle the black pudding for 2–3 minutes on each side until lovely and crisp. Serve the Scotch pancakes with the tomatoes, mushrooms and black pudding and a good dollop of mustard.

Irish Boxty

Boxty is a traditional Irish potato pancake made with a mixture of cooked, mashed and grated raw potato. Its texture is part pancake, part hash brown. In Gaelic, boxty translates as 'poor man's bread', as it was often served for breakfast in place of bread as an economical alternative. I can't help being amused by an old rhyme, 'Boxty on the griddle, boxty in the pan, if you can't make boxty, you'll never get a man'. My version is made with egg white and buttermilk for extra fluffiness, and with wholegrain mustard and chopped parsley for full on flavour has plenty of pulling power! I like to serve boxty with poached smoked haddock, spinach, poached eggs and a mustardy crème fraîche sauce to finish, for an Irish-inspired breakfast or brunch.

PREP 20 mins

COOK 30 mins

TOTAL 50 mins

DIETARY

USE GLUTEN-FREE FLOUR; AND USE RICE FLOUR MILK IN PLACE OF BUTTERMILK

MAKES

16 x 8CM, SERVES 4

300g fluffy potatoes (such as red Desiree), coarsely grated
300g potatoes, peeled, cooked and mashed
350g plain flour, sifted
1 teaspoon baking powder
2 tablespoons unsalted butter, melted, plus extra for cooking
1 large egg white
175ml buttermilk
2 tablespoons wholegrain mustard
4 tablespoons chopped parsley leaves
1 tablespoons sunflower or rapeseed oil
sea salt and freshly ground black pepper

FOR THE HADDOCK AND EGGS
200ml semi-skimmed milk
4 fillets of undyed smoked haddock
25g butter, cut into cubes
a splash of white wine vinegar
4 large eggs
500g baby spinach

FOR THE SAUCE
200ml crème fraîche
4 teaspoons wholegrain mustard
juice of ½ lemon
a handful of parsley leaves, chopped

Preheat the oven to 100°C/gas mark ¼ and put baking tray in the oven to keep the pancakes warm while you make them. Put the grated potato in a fine-meshed sieve set over a medium bowl and add a little salt. Toss well to mix, then press the grated potatoes against the sides of the strainer to remove any liquid.

Add the grated potatoes to the mashed potatoes. Add the flour and baking powder, then mix gently. Season with plenty of pepper, then stir in the melted butter.

Lightly whisk the egg white in a medium bowl. Add the buttermilk and whisk again to combine. Fold into the potato and flour mixture until evenly incorporated. Add the mustard and parsley, and stir in gently.

Heat a large non-stick frying pan or griddle over a medium heat. The pan is hot enough when water sprinkled onto the surface bounces and splutters; it is too hot if it evaporates instantly. Once the pan is ready, add 1 tablespoon oil and a knob of butter, and melt it gently. Drop four dollops of batter from a little height to spread into freeform boxty in the pan about 1.5cm thick. Cook for 4 minutes or until the pancakes are golden and crisp on the outside. Flip over and cook on the other side until golden.

Transfer to the baking tray in the oven. Repeat with the remaining batter, adding more oil and butter to the pan as necessary.

Meanwhile, to prepare the haddock, pour the milk into a wide-based saucepan or frying pan and season with a little salt. Bring to a simmer and add the haddock, skin-side down. Put the cubes of butter on top and cook for 6–8 minutes until it is opaque and flakes easily. Remove from the milk to serve.

While the fish is poaching, bring a small frying pan of water to the boil, add a splash of vinegar, and carefully add the eggs leaving space between them. Cook for 2–5 minutes or until the white is set and the yolk is creamy or to your liking.

Meanwhile, put the spinach leaves in a colander over the sink. Carefully pour over boiling water straight from the kettle to wilt, then squeeze out as much water as possible using your hands or a wooden spoon. Set aside.

To make the sauce, put the crème fraîche in a small pan over a medium heat and add the mustard. Heat through, stirring, until it is smooth, then add the lemon juice and parsley.

Serve the boxty with the smoked haddock placed on top of the spinach and a poached egg on the side with a liberal helping of mustard and crème fraîche sauce.

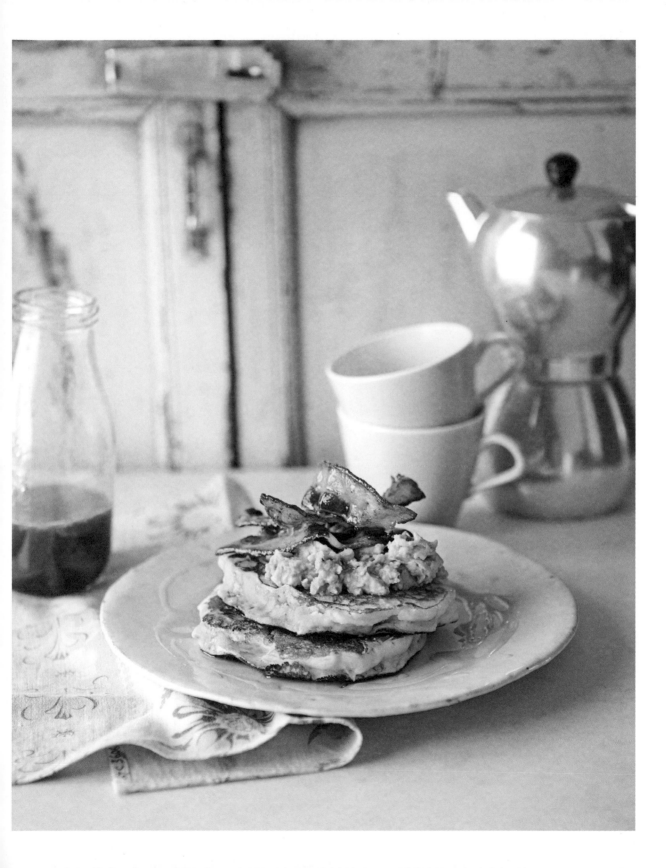

Fluffiest-Ever American Pancakes

WITH BACON, MAPLE SYRUP AND AVOCADO

For many of us, our obsession with pancakes began with discovering the greedy pleasures of American pancakes. The quintessential American-style pancake is ethereally light and fluffy, yet crisp on the outside and served in a 'devour-me' stack topped with bacon and an indecent amount of maple syrup cascading down its sides. What gives these pancakes such a brilliant texture is using a little baking powder and bicarbonate of soda, plus buttermilk. The bicarbonate of soda reacts with the acid in the batter mix to produce bubbles of carbon dioxide, which makes for a lighter-than-air finish. The most heavenly plump yet gossamer-light US pancakes I've ever eaten were from the Clinton Street Bakery in New York where they serve pancakes breakfast, noon and night, getting through more than 2,000 eggs in a week. Almost every order I saw emerge included pancakes. I follow owner Neil Kleinberg's advice to be extremely careful about how delicately I incorporate the egg whites into the batter, and that makes all the difference to their supreme fluffiness. At Clinton Street Bakery, the most popular pancake order is with blueberries. Never add blueberries to the batter; just scatter them on the top of the pancake as it cooks, and push them into the batter, otherwise the blueberries will bleed. At Clinton Street Bakery, pancakes are invariably served with the bakery's own maple salted-butter sauce, which is incredibly easy to replicate at home.

PREP 15 mins

COOK 15 mins

TOTAL 30 mins

DIETARY

USE GLUTEN-FREE PLAIN FLOUR

MAKES

8 x 12CM, SERVES 4

240g plain flour, sifted
2 teaspoons baking powder
1 teaspoon bicarbonate of soda
1 teaspoon salt
3 teaspoons golden caster sugar
500ml buttermilk
4 tablespoons butter, melted, plus 3 tablespoons
2 large eggs, separated
200g blueberries (optional)

FOR THE MAPLE SALTED-BUTTER SAUCE (optional)
125ml maple syrup
110g cold, unsalted butter, cubed

TO SERVE
8 rashers streaky bacon
2 avocados, halved, pitted and peeled
zest and juice of 1 lime
sea salt and freshly ground pepper
maple syrup, for drizzling

Preheat the oven to 120°C/gas mark ½ and put a baking tray with a wire rack inside in the oven for keeping the pancakes warm. In a large bowl, whisk together the flour, baking powder, bicarbonate of soda, salt and sugar. In a separate bowl gently whisk the buttermilk with the 4 tablespoons butter and the egg yolks. Put the egg whites in a clean, grease-free bowl and whisk until they form medium peaks yet are still soft in the middle – do not over-whisk. Gently fold half the egg whites into the batter using the whisk at first and then a spatula, turning the bowl while folding. Add the remaining egg whites in the same way. The batter should be slightly lumpy for the best results, with large parts of egg white not fully incorporated.

Heat a non-stick crêpe pan over a medium heat until hot. The pan is hot enough when water sprinkled onto the surface bounces and splutters; it is too hot if it evaporates instantly. Turn the heat down to medium–low. Brush the pan with 1 tablespoon melted butter and wipe off any excess with kitchen paper. (Using butter ensures an extra-crisp finish.)

Drop 2–3 tablespoons of the batter into the pan from the tip of the tablespoon for each pancake. This is the stage to scatter on the blueberries, if using. Cook for 2 minutes or until bubbles start to form and pop on the surface of the pancake and it is slightly dry and airy around the edges and lightly golden underneath. Flip over and cook for 2 minutes or until lightly golden. Keep the pancakes warm on the rack in the oven. Repeat with the remaining batter, adding more butter to the pan as necessary.

Meanwhile, fry the bacon in a dry frying pan over a high heat, or under a preheated grill, for 5 minutes. Mash up the avocados with a fork, then mix in the lime zest and juice, and season with black pepper.

To make the maple salted-butter sauce, if using, heat the maple syrup in a small saucepan over a medium heat. Whisk in the cold butter until it is incorporated and the sauce is smooth. Remove from the heat and keep warm until ready to use.

Serve a stack of pancakes, topped with the smashed avocado, crisp bacon and an indecent amount of maple syrup drizzled over, or serve with the maple salted-butter sauce.

Poffertjes

The name *poffertjes* refers to the way the pancakes puff up as they're turned in their special *poffertjes* pan, which has lots of little dimple-like indentations. *Poffertjes* are an integral part of every Dutch celebration, and are a particular feature of Christmas markets with street vendors cooking them in huge trays. Written recipes first appeared in the mid 1700s, when they were made with only buckwheat flour, yeast and water, and were considered a poor man's meal. Eggs, milk and a little sugar were later additions. I prefer lighter *poffertjes* made with 50:50 wheat and buckwheat. Their light, spongy texture, crisp finish and slightly fermented taste is irresistible. A huge platter of hot *poffertjes*, served traditionally doused in icing sugar with melted butter, is a superb treat after a long wintery shopping spree or a walk in the park. Although the Dutch never eat them for breakfast, *poffertjes* make a heavenly indulgent sweet brunch dish, especially served with cranberry and orange compete and coconut yogurt.

PREP 10 mins

plus 1 hour resting

COOK 10 mins

TOTAL 20 mins

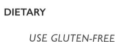

DIETARY

USE GLUTEN-FREE FLOURS

MAKES

ABOUT 40 x 3CM, SERVES 6

1 teaspoon, or 7g fast-action yeast
250ml warm milk
100g buckwheat flour
100g plain flour
pinch of salt
1 teaspoon golden caster sugar
2 large eggs
30g butter, melted

20g icing sugar

FOR THE COMPOTE
2 tablespoons soft brown sugar
3 organic oranges, blood oranges if available, peeled and sliced
250g cranberries, fresh or frozen
300ml coconut yogurt, optional

Preheat the oven to 100°C/gas mark ¼ and warm a plate.

Mix the yeast with 3 tablespoons of the warm milk and stir until dissolved. Sift the flours and salt into a large bowl, and add the sugar, yeast mixture and eggs. Combine well, then gradually add the remaining milk, whisking well between each addition until the batter is smooth and the consistency of double cream. Leave to rest, covered with clingfilm, for at least 1 hour.

After resting, stir the batter again. Ideally, use a funnel to fill a small squeezy bottle with the batter, which will make it easier to fill the shallow hollows of the pan. Believe me, this is very pleasing and makes things far less messy.

Heat the *poffertjes* pan over a medium–high heat, then quickly brush each indentation with melted butter. When the butter is sizzling, squirt in enough batter to fill each indentation or use a tablespoon or ladle dexterously. Cook for 1 minute, until bubbles start to form and pop on the surface and they become crisp at the edges. Deftly and rapidly turn the *poffertjes* using two forks. The underneath should be puffy and lightly golden. Cook for 1 minute. To serve traditionally, simply pile *poffertjes* onto a warm plate, dredge with icing sugar and anoint with melted butter. For a winter treat, add cranberry and orange compote and coconut yogurt.

For the compote, put the sugar and 2 tablespoons water in a pan and heat to dissolve the sugar. Once bubbling, add the orange and cranberries. Stir, then turn up the heat and leave to bubble for a few minutes until most of the liquid has evaporated and the compote is thick and sticky.

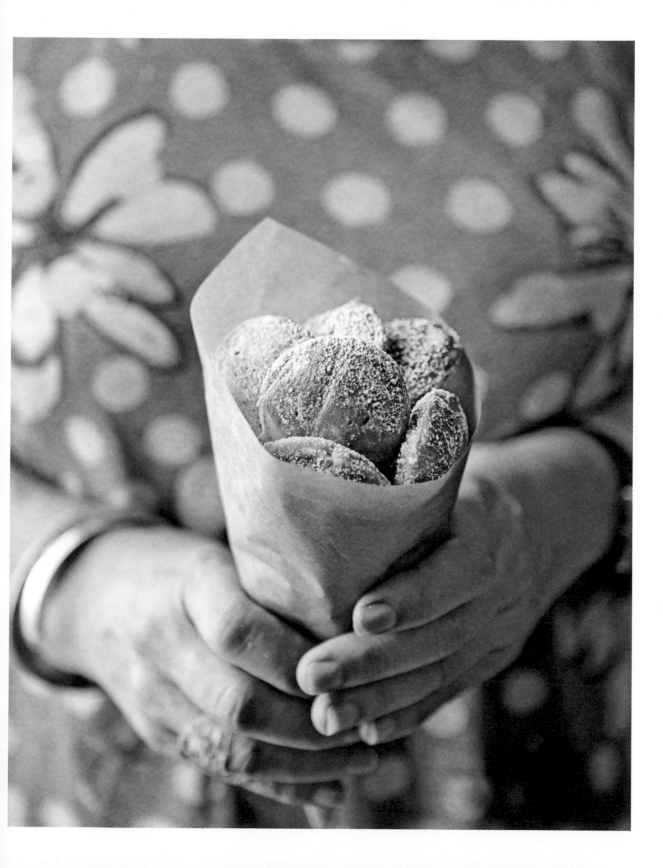

Potato Latkes

FRIED EGG, SUMAC, AVOCADO AND TAHINI HUMMUS

Potato pancakes are very much in vogue currently and it is difficult to resist their crisp, brown, wonderfully crunchy temptation. For me they are synonymous with my childhood. My great-grandmother would make incredible latkes to celebrate Hanukkah, the Jewish festival of lights commemorating Judah Maccabee recapturing the Holy Temple in Jerusalem in 164BC after it had been desecrated by the Syrian King Antiochus III. Miraculously, the flame for the eternal lamp continued to burn for eight days even though there scarcely seemed enough oil for one day. Hence, the treat of latkes fried in copious oil.

In my family, there's much dispute as to whether the potatoes should be grated or shredded in a food processor. Call me old-fashioned, but I still prefer to grate them. There's also heated discussion as to whether the potatoes should have their starch rinsed out, or collected in a strainer and returned to the pan. I tend to dispense with the starch. Latkes make a good sidekick to roast chicken or baked salmon, too, although for a snack or appetiser it is hard to beat the traditional (and, for me, nostalgic) accompaniments of cinnamon-scented apple sauce and soured cream. If you find yourself in New York, don't miss the latkes at Russ & Daughters served with smoked salmon and soured cream. For a rather different twist, Alsatian potato pancake recipes are made like latkes adding nutmeg and parsley to the mix. I also like Polish ratzelech: potato pancakes served with herring, beetroot and horseradish.

PREP 30 mins

COOK 20 mins

TOTAL 50 mins

DIETARY

USE GLUTEN-FREE FLOUR

MAKES

12 x 9CM,
SERVES 4

4 large potatoes
1 onion
3 tablespoons chopped parsley leaves
1 large egg, lightly beaten
2 tablespoons plain flour
½ teaspoon baking powder
salt and freshly ground pepper
sunflower oil or rapeseed oil, for cooking

FOR THE FRIED EGGS
4 tablespoons olive oil
4 large eggs
juice of 1 lemon
a sprinkle of sumac

FOR THE AVOCADO HUMMUS

1 avocado, halved, pitted and peeled
zest and juice of ½ lemon
400g can chickpeas, drained and rinsed
2 tablespoons tahini
1 garlic clove, crushed
3 tablespoons finely chopped coriander leaves
3 tablespoons olive oil, plus extra if needed

To make the avocado and tahini hummus, whizz all the ingredients in a food processor until they are incorporated into a thick, slightly whippy texture. Depending on the ripeness of the avocado, it might be necessary to add a little more olive oil or water.

Coarsely grate the potatoes and onion, alternating between onion and potato, as the acid in the onion helps to prevent the potato from discolouring. Transfer the potato mixture to a colander, and squeeze the mixture by hand to remove as much liquid as possible (this is really important, as the latkes won't crisp up if they are too watery). Transfer the mixture to a large bowl, and stir in the parsley, egg, flour and baking powder, then season with salt and pepper.

Heat 2 tablespoons oil in a large non-stick pan over a medium heat until it is shimmering. Spoon 2 tablespoons of the potato mixture into the pan for each latke. Flatten with the back of a spoon so that each is about 8–10cm in diameter. Fry for 4 minutes or until golden underneath and crisp. Turn the latkes carefully using 2 spatulas so that the oil doesn't splatter, and cook for 4 minutes until golden and crisp. It is a good idea to stir the potato mixture between frying the batches.

While the latkes are cooking, make the fried eggs with sumac. Heat a heavy frying pan over a medium–high heat and add 2 tablespoons of the oil. Cook 2 eggs at a time. Crack the eggs into the pan, wait until the whites are setting a little and then squeeze a little lemon juice over each, taking care, as it may splatter. Cook until set. Sprinkle with sumac before serving.

Shakshuka Quinoa & Buckwheat Pancakes

WITH EGGS AND HARISSA YOGURT

Strictly speaking, shakshuka is a tomato- and pepper-rich vegetable stew baked with egg. Enjoyed throughout the Middle East and Tunisia, it has become an insanely popular brunch dish with its potent mix of spicy flavours, thanks largely to chef Yotam Ottolenghi. I've taken liberties and used a shakshuka-inspired sauce with smoked paprika inside quinoa flour and buckwheat crêpes with harissa-spiked yogurt and a poached egg to make a more substantial, all-round brunch dish. The crepe-like pancakes have a distinctive earthiness about them which contrasts well with the shakshuka.

PREP 20 mins

★ plus 30 mins resting

COOK 30 mins

TOTAL 50 mins

DIETARY

QUINOA AND
BUCKWHEAT FLOUR
ARE GLUTEN-FREE

MAKES

8 x 24CM,
SERVES 4

100g quinoa flour
50g buckwheat flour
pinch of salt
2 large eggs, beaten
300ml semi-skimmed milk
20g unsalted butter, melted
sunflower oil or rapeseed oil, for
cooking
a splash of vinegar
4 eggs
salt and freshly ground pepper

FOR THE SHAKSHUKA
1 teaspoon cumin seeds
2 tablespoons extra virgin olive oil
1 onion, thinly sliced
1 red pepper and 1 green pepper,
deseeded and diced

2 garlic cloves, crushed
2 teaspoons smoked paprika
a large pinch of saffron threads
pinch of cayenne pepper, or to taste
400g tin tomatoes, or ripe fresh
tomatoes
2 teaspoons sugar
a large bunch of coriander, leaves finely
chopped
salt and freshly ground black pepper

FOR THE HARISSA YOGURT
2 teaspoons harissa paste
1 tablespoon lemon juice
1 garlic clove, crushed
1 tablespoon olive oil
a large bunch of parsley, finely chopped
250ml Greek yogurt

Preheat the oven to 100°C/gas mark ¼ and heat a plate to keep the pancakes warm while you make them.

Sift the flours and salt into a bowl. Make a well in the centre. Whisk in the eggs one at a time using an electric or hand whisk to give a thick, smooth batter. Gradually whisk in the milk, followed by the melted butter. Leave to rest for 30 minutes.

Meanwhile, to make the shakshuka, dry roast the cumin seeds in a large saucepan over a medium heat, tossing regularly until they begin to pop. Add the olive oil and onion, and cook for 5 minutes or until golden. Add the peppers and cook until soft. Stir in the garlic and the remaining spices and herbs. Cook for a further 3 minutes.

Add the tomatoes and sugar, then mash them down with a wooden spoon and bring them to the boil. Reduce the heat and simmer for 20 minutes or until the consistency of a thick pasta sauce. Season with salt and pepper. Add more cayenne for a spicier finish, if you like, and stir in the coriander.

To make the harissa yogurt, put the harissa paste in a small bowl and add the lemon juice, garlic, oil, parsley and yogurt. Whisk together, then set aside.

While the shakshuka is cooking, make the pancakes. Put a large frying pan over a medium heat. Use kitchen paper to wipe the pan with a good coating of sunflower oil. Pour a small ladleful of batter into the middle of the pan, tilting it quickly so that the batter covers the base thinly. Reduce the heat a little and cook for 1–2 minutes until almost set, bubbles start to form and pop on the surface and the underneath is pale golden. Flip over with a spatula and cook until pale golden – the second side will cook slightly more quickly. Turn out of the pan. Repeat with the remaining batter, adding more oil to the pan as necessary. Stack the pancakes on the warmed plate, interleaved with greaseproof paper.

Meanwhile, make the poached eggs. Bring a small frying pan of water to the boil, add a splash of vinegar, and carefully add the eggs leaving space between them. Cook for 2–5 minutes or until the white is set and the yolk is creamy or to your liking. Lift from the pan using a slotted spoon to serve.

Lay the pancakes out on a flat surface. Put 2 spoonfuls of shakshuka sauce in the middle of each crêpe, tuck the sides in and roll up. Serve with the harissa yogurt spooned over and the poached eggs alongside.

Snacks & Nibbles

Socca

Socca, made with chickpea flour, olive oil and water, is so simple, and so redolent of sunny Nice and the Riviera. I especially like it with homemade anchoïade and crème fraîche, though pistou or tapenade are great accompaniments too. I first tried it in Nice's Cours Saleya market – the socca is whizzed there from a bakery deep in the Old Town on the back of a bicycle, and it smells so enticing. Chez Pipo on the edge of Nice Old Town, however, is the real deal. Here the socca is cooked over a mightily impressive wood fire and has a satisfyingly deep, earthy, smoky tang. I am impressed, however, by just how good socca made in a frying pan tastes, especially with the addition of a generous teaspoon of cumin, which adds toasty notes that hint at a wood fire. Folding in two egg whites makes for a lighter socca, although it is not essential and definitely not how the Niçoise make it.
In Nice market, socca is served cut into triangles and sprinkled with sea salt. I find it makes a rather good pre-dinner or party snack. It is extra-good with a special seaweed salt, or even a truffle salt.

PREP 15 mins

*plus 30 mins resting

COOK 20 mins

TOTAL 35 mins

DIETARY

CHICKPEA FLOUR IS
GLUTEN-FREE

MAKES

12–16 x 9CM,
OR 4 LARGE,
SERVES 4

1½ tablespoons olive oil, plus extra for greasing
250g chickpea flour (gram flour)
½ teaspoon salt
a good grinding of black pepper
½ teaspoon ground cumin
500ml tepid water
2 large egg whites

FOR THE ANCHOÏADE
100g jar of anchovies, drained
1 garlic clove, crushed
a good handful of flat-leaf parsley leaves
3–4 tablespoons olive oil

To make the anchoïde, put the anchovies, garlic and parsley in a food processor and whizz, adding the olive oil gradually until it becomes a rough, thick paste. Set aside.

Preheat the oven to 100°C/gas mark ¼ and line two baking trays with greaseproof paper, then brush them lightly with olive oil. Put the chickpea flour in a large bowl and mix in the salt, pepper and cumin. Gradually pour in the water, whisking with an electric hand-held beater as you go. Continue whisking until the mixture is smooth and the consistency of double cream. Put the egg whites into a clean bowl and whisk until just stiff. Gently incorporate the egg whites into the socca mixture using a metal spoon. Don't be tempted to use a whisk. Leave to rest in the fridge for at least 30 minutes, or even prepare it first thing in the morning ready for the evening.

Place a non-stick frying pan over a high heat for 2 minutes, then reduce the heat to medium–high. Using a heatproof pastry brush, brush the pan with olive oil. Pour a ladleful of batter into the pan, the socca should be about 5mm thick. Cook for 2 minutes or until tiny bubbles start to form on the surface. Flip over and cook for 2 minutes or until lightly golden, a little crisp and lacy. Transfer to the warmed baking trays while you repeat with the remaining batter, adding more oil to the pan as necessary. Serve with bowls of anchoïade and crème fraîche for diners to dollop onto their socca. Accompany with a crisp salad and a well-chilled glass of rosé for instant transportation to Nice.

Farinata

WITH ROSEMARY AND SEA SALT OR PESTO

Traditionally, *farinata*, a baked chickpea pancake, is made in a wood-fired oven, although it works well started on the hob and finished in the oven. I adore it as an appetiser or as a simple supper with a robust green salad, some charcuterie and cheese, especially crumbled Gorgonzola. Usually, it is just sprinkled with red onion, rosemary and sea salt, and it's fantastic with a crisp Soave or cold Italian beer. As the dish originates in Genoa, where the fishermen often eat it for breakfast in the early hours before setting out to sea, I also like to stir in some homemade pesto, which makes for an even more striking-looking and tasting *farinata*. Buy the best-quality chickpea flour you can source, preferably an Italian brand, for the tastiest of *farinata*. It will be called *farina di ceci*. Chickpea flour is now found in the Indian sections of supermarkets (under gram flour) and good delis.

PREP 10 mins

* plus 4 hours or overnight resting

COOK 20 mins

TOTAL 30 mins

DIETARY

CHICKPEA FLOUR IS GLUTEN-FREE

MAKES

2 x 24CM, SERVES 4–6

1 litre sparkling water
2 teaspoons cooking salt
300g chickpea flour, sifted
100ml extra virgin olive oil
1 red onion, quartered and sliced into ultra-thin slivers
leaves from 2 large sprigs of rosemary
sea salt, to sprinkle

FOR THE BASIL PESTO
50g pine nuts
50g Parmesan, finely grated
1 garlic clove, crushed
75g basil leaves
salt and freshly ground pepper
125ml good-quality extra virgin olive oil

Pour the sparkling water into a bowl and add the salt and chickpea flour with 1½ tablespoons of the olive oil. Stir with a whisk to form a thick batter. Leave the mixture to stand at room temperature in a warmish place for 4–5 hours or, better still, overnight, so that the mixture can start fermenting, which gives the pancake a light, airy texture.

Preheat the oven to 200°C/gas mark 6.

To make the pesto, if using this alternative, heat a small pan over a medium–high heat and add the pine nuts. Cook to brown evenly, shaking the pan from time to time. Remove the pine nuts, retaining a few for garnish, and put the rest into a blender or food processor with the Parmesan, garlic, basil leaves and seasoning. Whizz briefly. With the motor still running, gradually add the oil to make a smooth pesto. Set aside.

Heat a large, heavy ovenproof frying pan over a medium–high heat until it's almost smoking. Using a heatproof pastry brush, brush the base generously with olive oil. Pour in the batter until no more than 7mm thick, and swirl it around so that the batter spreads out evenly. Cook for 1–2 minutes – the mixture will begin to bubble. Scatter over the onion slices and rosemary, or stir in 4–5 tablespoons of pesto and top with a scattering of pine nuts. Transfer the farinata to the oven for 10–12 minutes until set and the edges are crispy. Repeat with the remaining mixture. Serve sprinkled with sea salt and cut into wedges.

Blinis

WITH SMOKED SALMON, HORSERADISH AND SOURED CREAM

Homemade blinis are a world apart from what the supermarkets offer up. They are warm, soft, doughy, fragrant, yeasty and light. Authentic Russian blinis are made with buckwheat, which is not wheat at all, but a member of the rhubarb family and has a slightly sour, nutty edge. I find it rather heavy used by itself, so tend to use a quarter buckwheat to three-quarters plain flour. In Russia and other Eastern European countries blinis are served at the beginning of Russian Orthodox Lent. The tradition dates back to pagan times when Maslenitsa, or the sun festival, was celebrated to mark the coming of spring. Round and golden blinis were thought to symbolise the sun and bring warmth.

PREP 15 mins

* plus 30 mins resting

COOK 15 mins

TOTAL 30 mins

DIETARY

USE GLUTEN-FREE FLOUR

MAKES

20 x 7CM, SERVES 4–6

50g butter
175ml semi-skimmed milk
170g plain flour (or use 40g buckwheat flour and 130g plain flour, if you like), sifted
2 sachets fast-acting yeast
pinch of golden caster sugar
2 large eggs, separated
butter, for cooking

TO SERVE

300g soured cream, smetana (Russian cultured cream) or crème fraîche
3 tablespoons creamed or grated fresh horseradish
200g smoked salmon
a small bunch of dill
caviar (optional) (true Beluga or salmon roe, depending on budget)

Preheat the oven to 100°C/gas mark ¼ and put in a rack on a baking tray to keep the blinis warm.

Melt the butter in a small pan over a medium heat, stir in the milk and set aside. In a large bowl, mix together the flour, yeast and sugar. Pour in the milk mixture. Beat the egg yolks lightly, then mix them gently into the batter. It will feel quite elastic. Set aside for 30 minutes at room temperature to ferment a little. Put the egg whites into a clean bowl and whisk until stiff and fluffy. Carefully and gently fold them into the batter.

Warm a non-stick frying pan or blini pan over a medium heat and use kitchen paper to smear on a little butter. Put 2 heaped tablespoons of batter into the pan, then use the tip of the spoon to spread it into a circle. I make each about 6–7cm in diameter. Add more batter to make 2–3 more pancakes in the pan at the same time. Leave them to spread, rise and cook for up to 1 minute or until pale golden underneath. Flip over and cook for 40 seconds or until lightly golden. Keep warm in the oven and repeat with the remaining batter, adding more butter to the pan as necessary. (They can be wrapped up in parcels of foil to reheat, too.)

Mix the soured cream with the horseradish in a small bowl. Serve the blinis in a generous pile with the smoked salmon and horseradish soured cream separately for constructing DIY blinis. Alternatively, spoon a little horseradish soured cream on top of each blini, top with strips of smoked salmon and sprigs of dill. If you're feeling flush, proffer caviar too!

Potato Blinis

A dreamy, wispy-light alternative to proper fermented blinis or more substantial potato pancakes, my potato blini recipe was first created by a chef–consultant friend, Philip Owens. Using fluffy baking potatoes is essential and they need to be baked for a good hour before making the blinis to ensure that they have the mesmerising lightness. Philip always serves these with smoked eel, crisp bacon and horseradish cream at Christmas before roast goose. For a summer party, I have adapted the recipe and topped with a delicately spiced crab cocktail.

PREP 10 mins

plus 30 mins resting

COOK 75 mins

TOTAL 85 mins

DIETARY

USE GLUTEN-FREE
PLAIN FLOUR

MAKES

20 x 5CM,
SERVES 4–6

300g baking potatoes
2 large eggs, beaten, plus 2 egg whites
60ml double cream
60ml semi-skimmed milk
1½ tablespoons plain flour
butter, for cooking
200ml crème fraîche, to serve

FOR THE CRAB COCKTAIL TOPPING
1 dressed crab, or 200g crabmeat

zest of 1 lime and 3 tablespoons lime juice
½ red chilli, deseeded and finely chopped
1 tablespoon finely chopped chives
1 tablespoon finely chopped flat-leaf parsley
1 tablespoon extra virgin olive oil
sea salt and freshly ground black pepper

Preheat the oven to 200°C/gas mark 6. Bake the potatoes for 1 hour or until the insides are soft. Remove from the oven. Turn the oven down to 100°C/gas mark ¼ and put a rack on a baking tray inside to keep the blinis warm.

Meanwhile, put the crabmeat in a bowl and mix in the lime zest and juice, chilli, herbs and olive oil. Season with salt and pepper. Keep in the fridge until ready to use.

Push the cooked potato through a potato ricer or sieve into a bowl or food processor. Mix with the 2 beaten eggs, cream, milk, flour and ½ teaspoon salt, either in the food processor or using an electric whisk. Tip into a large mixing bowl. Put the egg whites in a clean, grease-free bowl and whisk until they form soft peaks. Gently fold into the potato mixture using a spatula. Leave to rest in a cool place for 30 minutes.

Place a large non-stick frying pan on a medium–high heat. Add 1 teaspoon butter and swirl to coat the pan. Drop in tablespoonfuls of batter from the tip of a tablespoon, as many as will fit at one time. It will sizzle as it hits the pan. Cook for 2 minutes or until lightly golden. Flip over and cook for a further 2 minutes, then keep warm in the oven. Repeat with the remaining batter, adding a little more butter to the pan as necessary.

The potato pancakes can also be made in advance and reheated in a preheated oven at 100°C/gas mark ¼ on a baking tray lined with greaseproof paper. If doing this, allow the pancakes to cool a little before topping them with crème fraîche, otherwise this will melt and run off. Top with a dollop of crème fraîche and the crab cocktail then serve.

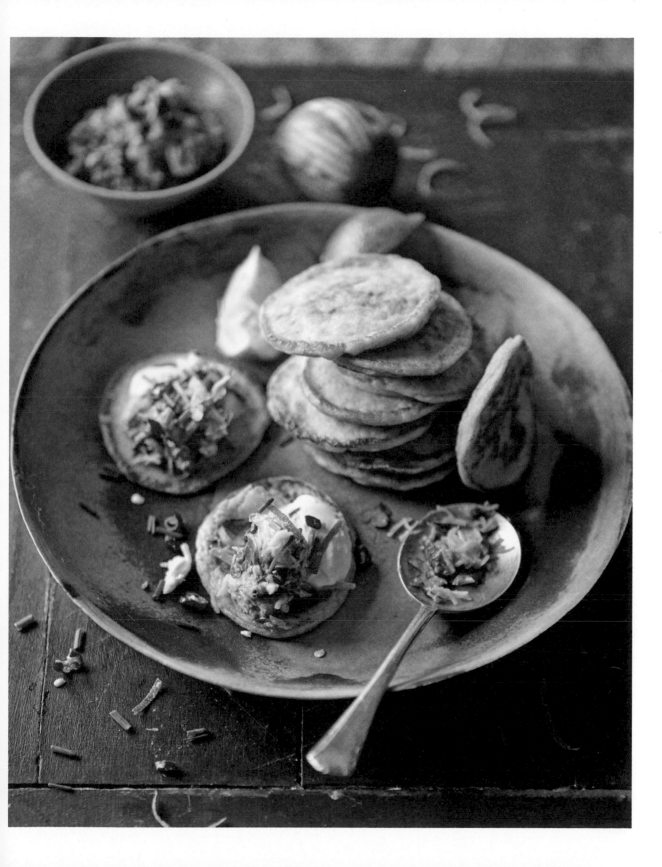

Cong You Bing

SPRING ONION PANCAKE

Rich, crisp and addictively moreish, these green-onion pancakes are one of Northern China's most famous street foods, often found at breakfast 'shops' or on dim sum menus. They are made with a dough of flour and hot water, rather than a batter, and shaped into snail-like coils and rolled to give them their distinctive flaky texture. Serve with a dipping sauce made with soy sauce, rice wine vinegar and lime as a party snack or for a light supper.

PREP 30 mins

* plus 30 mins resting

COOK 30 mins

TOTAL 60 mins

DIETARY

USE GLUTEN-FREE FLOUR

MAKES

16 x 8CM,
SERVES 8 AS A SNACK,
2 AS A MAIN MEAL

½ teaspoon sea salt

275g plain flour, sifted, plus extra for dusting

sunflower oil

2 tablespoons toasted sesame oil

1 bunch of spring onions, green parts and a little of the white finely chopped

1 tablespoon Chinese five-spice powder (optional)

FOR THE DIPPING SAUCE

4 tablespoons rice wine vinegar

4 tablespoons good soy sauce

3cm piece of fresh ginger, peeled and finely grated

½ teaspoon dried chilli flakes

1 teaspoon golden caster sugar

juice of 1 lime

In a bowl, dissolve the salt in 175ml hand-hot water and mix with the flour to form a soft dough. Turn out onto a well-floured surface and knead for at least 5 minutes until the dough is very smooth and slightly springy. Divide into 8 balls (or 16 if you wish to serve as party snack), brush very lightly with oil, put in a bowl covered with a damp tea-towel, and leave to rest for 30 minutes.

Meanwhile, mix the rice wine vinegar in a jug with the soy sauce, ginger, chilli flakes, sugar and lime juice, then divide into individual bowls ready to serve. Set aside.

On a floured surface, roll out each ball into a thin rectangle about 12 x 18cm. Brush with sesame oil and sprinkle with the spring onion and five-spice powder, if using. Starting at the long end, roll the dough into a cigar shape, brush the inside with a little more sesame oil, then roll into a snail shape and tuck under the ends. Press lightly with your hands to flatten the spiral. Roll it out very gently into an ultra-thin pancake. You should still see the coils. Roll gently to retain flakiness and turn often to avoid making holes in the pancakes. Cover the prepared pancakes with a damp cloth. Repeat with the remaining dough.

Heat a non-stick frying pan over a medium heat and brush with sunflower oil. When the oil is shimmering, slip the first pancake into the hot pan. It should sizzle and not burn. Cook for 2 minutes or until golden, shaking the pan gently. Flip over and cook for 2 minutes or until golden. Drain on a plate covered with kitchen paper. Repeat with the remaining pancake coils. Serve warm with the dipping sauce.

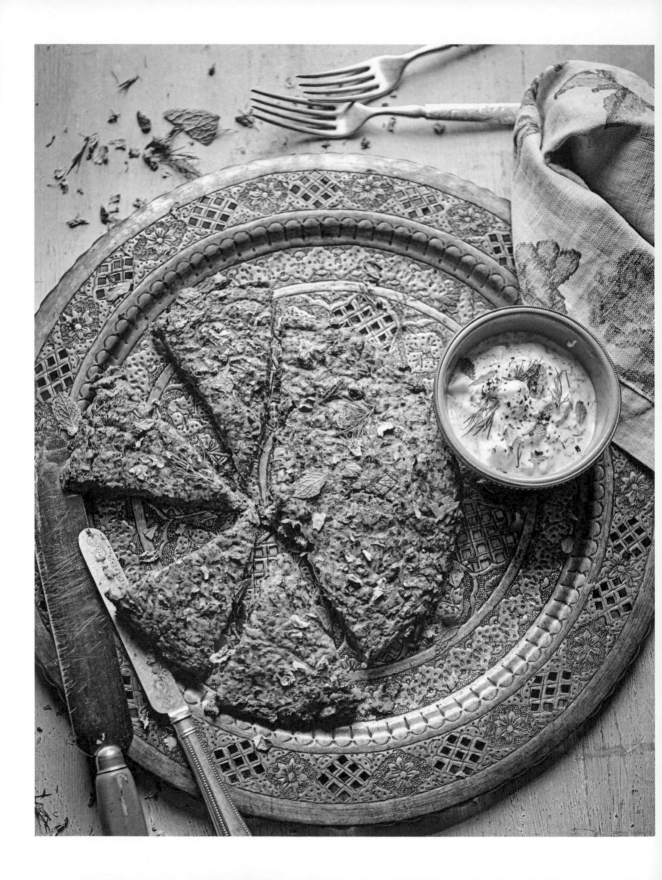

Kuku Sibzamini

PERSIAN-STYLE SAFFRON AND SWEET POTATO PANCAKE

A Persian egg-based frittata, *kuku* is eaten at New Year in Iran. The herbs symbolise rebirth, and the eggs promise fertility and happiness for the year to come. When made with potato, it is called *kuku sibzamini*. I've long adored sweet potato, and using it here gives the pancake a slightly different, richer flavour. I've scented it with saffron, which raises the dish to another level of intense flavour. The addition of walnuts for an interesting crunch, and tiny Iranian barberries for a refreshing sour zing, is traditional and adds surprise.
I make one large *kuku sibzamini* and my preference is to serve it warm or at room temperature cut into wedges with cool yogurt mixed with cucumber and lots of fresh mint, dill and parsley.

PREP 15 mins

COOK 30 mins

TOTAL 45 mins

DIETARY

GLUTEN-FREE

MAKES

1 x 24CM,
SERVES 6 AS A SNACK,
2 AS A MAIN MEAL

500g sweet potato, unpeeled and cut into quarters
½ teaspoon saffron threads
3 large eggs
2 tablespoons plain flour
2 teaspoons baking powder
½ teaspoon bicarbonate of soda
1 garlic clove, crushed
a large bunch of parsley, finely chopped
a large bunch of mint, finely chopped
a large bunch of dill, finely chopped
20g chervil (optional), finely chopped
20g tarragon (optional), finely chopped

50g walnuts, finely chopped
50g barberries, soaked, rinsed and dried on kitchen paper
sunflower oil or rapeseed oil
sea salt and freshly ground black pepper

FOR THE YOGURT SAUCE
8 tablespoons Greek yogurt
½ cucumber peeled, and diced
a large handful each of fresh parsley, mint and dill, leaves finely chopped
rose petals, to decorate (optional)

Bring a pan of salted water to the boil and cook the potato for 10–15 minutes until fork-tender. Cool a little, remove the skins, then mash. Crush the saffron using a pestle and mortar, then put it in a small bowl and add 1 tablespoon boiling water. Leave to soak.

Put the eggs in a bowl and sift in the flour, baking powder and bicarbonate of soda. Add the garlic, herbs, saffron in its liquid, walnuts and barberries. Season with salt and pepper, then stir in the mashed sweet potatoes.

Heat a little oil in a large, heavy frying pan over a medium heat until it begins to sizzle, then reduce the heat and pour in all the *kuku* batter. Cook for 1 minute, then loosen the kuku around the edges. Cover with a lid and continue to cook over a low heat for 20–30 minutes or until the *kuku* is just set and still fluffy within. Cut into wedges.

To make the sauce, put the yogurt in a bowl and add the cucumber and herbs. Season with salt and pepper, then mix together well. Pour the yogurt sauce over the *kuku* and garnish with dried rose petals for an optional added flourish, if you like.

Main Meals

Farçous

SWISS CHARD PANCAKES WITH LEMON BERBERE BUTTER

Farçou comes from Aveyron in south-west France, although it is a popular staple throughout the region. It has the texture of a thick crêpe and tastes hugely healthy as it is loaded with greens, specifically Swiss chard, plus masses of herbs (usually parsley and chives) and garlic. As an accompaniment, I created a lemon berbere – an Ethiopian hot spice that is available ready blended (containing chilli, garlic, ginger, cardamom, clove and fenugreek) – butter accompaniment. The French generally serve *farçous* as a robust main meal – either as small fritters or a large frying-pan-sized *farçou* – with salad. I recommend one of bitter leaves, Roquefort and walnuts to stay with the south-west French flavours. The batter will keep in the fridge for 2 days. Cooked *farçous* even taste good cold the next day if any are leftover. They also freeze well, wrapped in greaseproof paper for up to 1 month.

PREP 10 mins
plus 1 hour chilling

COOK 20 mins

TOTAL 40 mins

DIETARY

USE GLUTEN-FREE
PLAIN FLOUR

MAKES

16 x 8CM,
SERVES 4

150g plain flour, sifted
6 spring onions, finely chopped
250ml semi-skimmed milk
2 large eggs
8 Swiss chard leaves, tougher stems discarded, finely chopped
2 garlic cloves, crushed
a small bunch of flat-leaf parsley, finely chopped
10 chives, finely chopped
sprinkle of freshly grated nutmeg

salt and freshly ground black pepper
sunflower oil or rapeseed oil

FOR THE LEMON BERBERE BUTTER
100g unsalted butter, at room temperature
1 teaspoon berbere spice mix (Seasoned Pioneers do a good one)
zest of 1 lemon and 2 tablespoons lemon juice

To make the berbere butter, cream the butter in a small bowl. Add the spice, lemon zest and juice, season with salt and pepper, and mix well. Form into a long roll, then cover with clingfilm and put it in the freezer for 15 minutes or in the fridge for 1 hour to firm up.

Preheat the oven to 100°C/gas mark ¼, line a baking tray with foil and put it in the oven to keep the *farçous* warm while you make them.

Put the flour, spring onions, milk and eggs in a blender or food processor and whizz to make a batter. Add the Swiss chard and garlic and whizz briefly so there are still some longish strands of green leaves. Pour into a bowl and stir in the herbs, nutmeg and seasoning.

Place a large, non-stick frying pan over a medium heat. Smear generously with oil using kitchen paper, and heat until hot enough that a droplet of batter sizzles. Add 2 tablespoons of the batter to make small *farçous*, or you can make several pan-sized ones instead. Cook for 3 minutes or until lightly browned underneath and turning frilly at the edges. Flip over and cook for a further 2 minutes. Keep warm in the oven and repeat with the remaining batter, adding more oil to the pan as necessary. Serve with the lemon berbere butter.

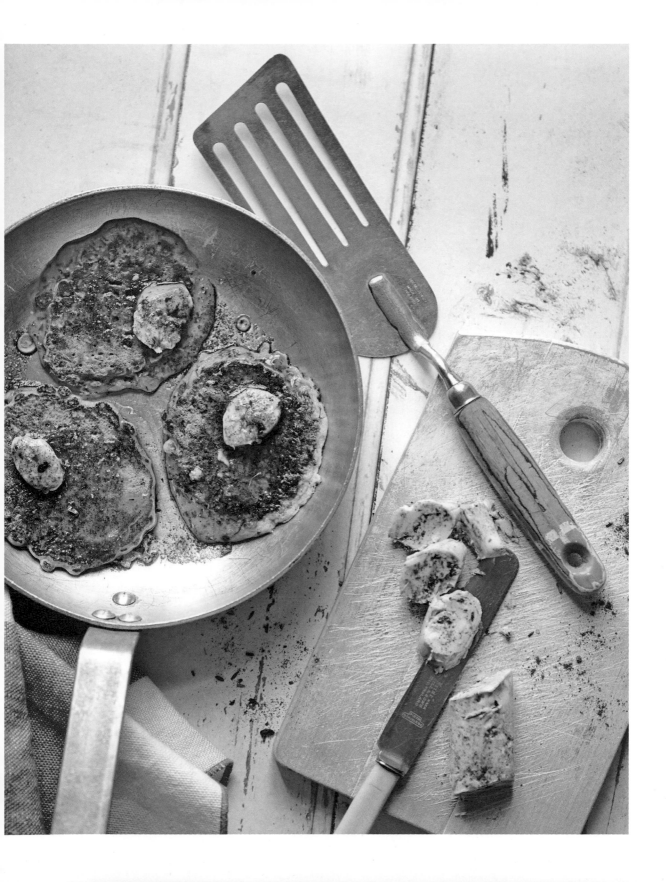

Crespelle

BAKED SPINACH AND RICOTTA CRESPELLE WITH TOMATO SAUCE

This is a truly comforting number featuring a classic Italian combination of spinach (do use fresh), ricotta and tomato. The crespelles should really be as thin as cannelloni. The velvety sauce thickens as it cooks.

PREP 30 mins

COOK 40 mins

TOTAL 70 mins

MAKES

8 x 24CM,
SERVES 4

120g plain flour
3 large eggs
200ml semi-skimmed milk
50g melted butter
1–2 tablespoons oil

FOR THE TOMATO SAUCE
1 tablespoon extra virgin olive oil
1 red onion, finely chopped
1 garlic clove, crushed
400g tin chopped tomatoes or passata
1 teaspoon golden caster sugar
20g basil leaves, shredded

FOR THE FILLING
1 tablespoon extra virgin olive oil
1 red onion, finely chopped
1 garlic clove, crushed
350g spinach
250g ricotta
zest of ½ lemon
30g anchovies in olive oil, chopped
40g Parmesan, grated
½ teaspoon freshly grated nutmeg

sea salt and freshly ground black
pepper

To make the tomato sauce, heat the oil in a small pan and cook the onion for 5 minutes or until soft. Add the garlic and cook for 1 minute. Add the tomatoes and sugar, and cook for 15–20 minutes until thick. Season to taste, then add the basil.

Meanwhile, to make the filling, heat the oil in a saucepan over a medium heat, add the onion and cook for 5 minutes or until soft. Add the garlic, cook for another 1 minute, then add the spinach. Reduce the heat, cover and cook gently for 2 minutes to wilt the spinach. Tip into a sieve over a bowl and press out any excess liquid. Transfer to another bowl, cool slightly and add the ricotta, lemon zest, anchovies, 30g of the Parmesan and the nutmeg. Season to taste.

While the sauce is cooking, put the flour and eggs in a large bowl and season with salt. Gradually whisk in the milk and butter until you have a smooth batter with the consistency of double cream. Pour into a jug. Preheat the oven to 180°C/gas mark 4.

Heat a large non-stick frying pan over a medium–high heat and add 1 tablespoon oil. Spread evenly with kitchen paper. Pour about 5 tablespoons of batter into the centre of the pan and immediately swirl it around so that it evenly covers the whole of the base. Cook for 2 minutes or until the top is set and the base is golden. Flip over and cook for 1 minute. Transfer to a plate. Repeat with the remaining batter, adding more oil to the pan as necessary. Put 2 tablespoons of the filling at the base of each pancake and roll up. Arrange the pancakes seam-side down in an oiled ovenproof dish. Spoon over the sauce, sprinkle over the remaining Parmesan and bake for 20–25 minutes until bubbling hot and a little crisp on top.

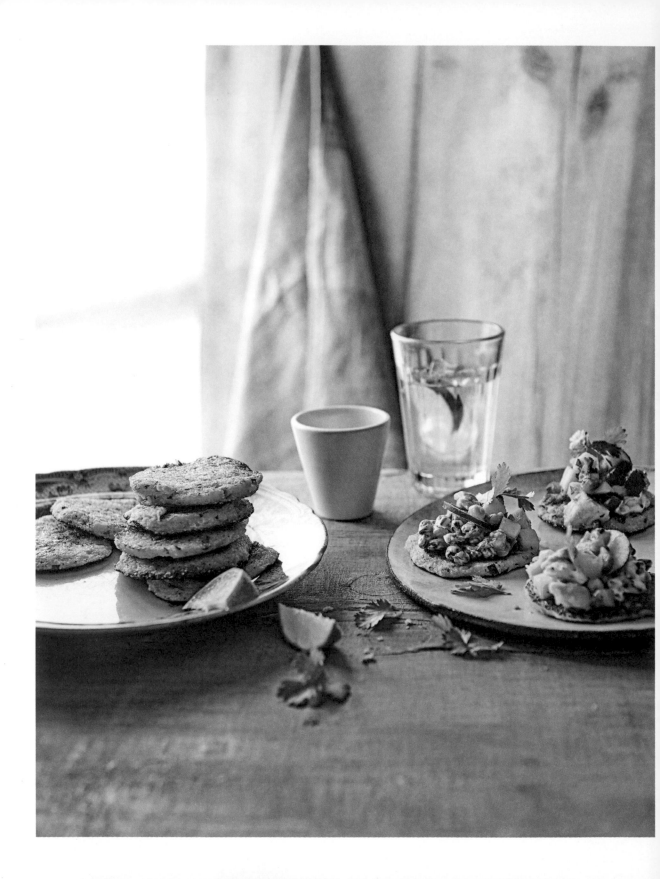

Arepas de Choclo

WITH BLACK BEANS, SPICY AVOCADO, MANGO AND TOMATO SALSA

These Colombian and Venezuelan pancakes are usually made from cornmeal and stuffed with cheese or served as a savoury 'sandwich', brimming with chicken and avocado, chorizo, plantain or black beans. The Venezuelans favour a thicker, rounded, palm-shaped arepa, split open and filled, whereas the Colombians prefer larger, floppier arepas that fold around fillings. Ideally, use a yellow or white masarepa maize flour that is pre-cooked (found in Colombian and Caribbean stores; a make called PAN Harina is popular). If you can't find it, instant, pre-cooked polenta works too and gives a rather appealing coarser texture, though the arepas don't end up so fluffy and thick.

PREP 30 mins

COOK 20 mins

TOTAL 50 mins

DIETARY

POLENTA AND
MASAREPA ARE BOTH
GLUTEN-FREE

MAKES

8 x 10CM,
SERVES 4

200g sweetcorn kernels, fresh or
frozen, cooked
250ml semi-skimmed milk
20g unsalted butter
200g pre-cooked polenta or marasepa
1 teaspoon golden caster sugar
125g mozzarella, grated
small bunch of coriander, chopped
½ green chilli, deseeded and finely
chopped
butter or corn oil, for cooking

FOR THE FILLING
400g can black beans, drained
1 teaspoon paprika

1 garlic clove, crushed
1 tablespoon avocado oil or olive oil
150ml soured cream
3 tablespoons chopped coriander

FOR THE SALSA
400g tomatoes, chopped
2 avocados, chopped
1 mango, chopped
1 green chilli, deseeded and chopped
zest and juice of 1 lime
8 radishes, finely sliced
a small bunch of coriander, chopped
2 tablespoons olive oil
sea salt and freshly ground pepper

Preheat the oven to 100°C/gas mark ¼ and heat a plate to keep the arepas warm.

Put the sweetcorn in a blender and add the milk. Pulse until the corn is roughly ground. Pour into a saucepan over a medium–high heat and add the butter. Heat until the milk is just boiling. Cool a little. Put the polenta in a bowl and mix in the sugar and ½ teaspoon salt. Add the mozzarella, coriander and chilli. Stir in the milk mixture (the polenta will absorb some of the liquid). Season. You'll have a thick pancake batter, not a pouring batter.

Mix the filling ingredients in a bowl. Mix the salsa ingredients together and season well.

Melt a small knob of butter in a large frying pan. Spoon in 3 tablespoons of batter to make a pancake about 12cm in diameter and 3cm thick. Press down gently using a spatula and cook for 2–3 minutes, until golden. Flip over and cook for 5–7 minutes. Keep warm. Repeat with the remaining batter, adding more butter to the pan as necessary. When ready, split an arepa through the centre without cutting right through, then fill with the bean mixture or pile beans on top of the arepa. Serve with the salsa.

Hoppers

I first came across these at Hoppers, the brilliant and massively popular Soho restaurant owned by the Sethi family, where queues form at each service for these pancakes. I was completely entranced by their filigree-thin, curved, bowl-shape, and the egg nestling in the middle.

Hoppers are Sri Lanka's favourite breakfast, and taste distinctively tangy and sweetly rich because they are fermented overnight and made with coconut milk and rice flour. They're gluten-free too. Despite being told that they are fiendishly hard to perfect, I was determined to master cooking them myself. The bowl shape comes from using a special hopper or *appam* pan. It's a good idea to locate an inexpensive non-stick one if you can – I found one at an Asian cookery shop. They're like small woks with outward-sloping sides and should come with a lid. Otherwise, a small non-stick wok or high-sided omelette pan with a lid works well. At Hoppers, they dip half an onion into sunflower oil and rub it around the hopper pan, which works most effectively in making the hoppers easy to remove. I would advise having at least one practice run when making hoppers before inviting guests over. For a more substantial meal, serve with a Sri Lankan chicken curry. I have given here a coconut sambol and an onion sambol alternative plus kiri hodi, a spinach 'gravy'.

PREP 45 mins
*plus 30 mins and overnight resting

COOK 30 mins

TOTAL 75 mins

DIETARY

RICE FLOUR IS
GLUTEN-FREE

MAKES

8 x 20CM,
SERVES 4

1 sachet fast-action yeast
400ml can coconut milk, shaken well
1 teaspoon golden caster sugar
200g brown rice flour, sifted, plus extra if needed
coconut oil, for cooking
8 large eggs
wedges of lime, chilli sauce and sprigs of fresh coriander, to serve

FOR THE COCONUT SAMBOL
1 green chilli, finely chopped
1 shallot, finely sliced
2 tablespoons coriander, finely chopped
2 teaspoons bonito flakes (optional)
200g grated coconut, (you can use fresh coconut pieces)
zest and juice of 1 lime
salt and freshly ground black pepper

FOR THE ONION SAMBOL
4 cardamom pods
4 tablespoons sunflower or rapeseed oil
4 whole cloves
4cm piece of cinnamon stick
500g red onions, finely sliced
1 green chilli, finely chopped
1 tablespoon lime juice
2 teaspoons sugar, or to taste

FOR THE KIRI HODI
1 red onion, sliced
2 garlic cloves, crushed
2.5cm piece of fresh ginger, grated
1 teaspoon ground turmeric
1 teaspoon ground fenugreek seeds
2.5cm piece of cinnamon stick
1 green chilli, finely chopped
6–8 fresh curry leaves, to taste
400ml can coconut milk, shaken well
125g baby spinach leaves, chopped
juice of ½ lime

Put the yeast in a bowl, add 100ml of the coconut milk and the sugar, and whisk to combine. Leave to stand for 30 minutes or until the batter begins to bubble, then add the remaining coconut milk and 100ml warm water. Put the rice flour in a large bowl. Make a well in the centre and pour in the yeasty coconut liquid. Whisk until smooth to make a thin batter. Add a little more warm water if necessary. Cover the bowl with clingfilm, and leave at room temperature overnight.

The next day, to make the coconut sambol, put the chilli in a blender and add the shallot, coriander and bonito flakes, if using, and 1 teaspoon salt. Whizz to a smooth paste. Tip into a bowl, add the grated coconut, a good grinding of black pepper and the lime zest and juice. Stir well, then cover and chill.

To make the onion sambol, bash the cardamom pods in a pestle and mortar. Heat the oil in a frying pan and add the cardamom, cloves and cinnamon. When the spices smell aromatic, add the onions, chilli and 1 teaspoon salt, then cook over a medium–low heat for 30–40 minutes, stirring occasionally to ensure the onions don't burn. Stir in the lime juice and sugar to taste, then cook until the sugar has dissolved. Check the seasoning and remove from the heat.

Put all the ingredients for the kiri hodi, except the spinach and lime juice, in a saucepan set over a medium heat and simmer for 15 minutes or until the onions have softened and the sauce has thickened. Tip in the spinach and stir to wilt. Remove from the heat. Season to taste with salt and add the lime juice. Remove the cinnamon stick and curry leaves. Keep warm.

Stir the hopper batter, add 1 teaspoon salt, and a little more warm water to loosen it if it is too thick. It should be the consistency of single cream. Heat a hopper pan over a medium– high heat, then add 1 tablespoon coconut oil and tip the pan to coat it in the oil, removing any excess using kitchen paper. Working quickly, add a ladleful of batter to the pan, then immediately hold the pan by its handles and swirl it in a circular motion to make a thin pancake that coats the base and sides of the pan. A hopper should have a thin, lacy layer of batter sticking to the sides with a slightly thicker layer in the centre. If the hopper batter doesn't stick to the sides of the pan, whisk in a few extra tablespoons of rice flour for the next round. Or use a spoon to add extra batter to the sides. When the outside of the hopper is just beginning to set, crack an egg into the centre and cover the pan with a lid. Cook for 2 minutes or until the egg white has set and the hopper is crisp and golden. The egg yolk should still be slightly creamy in the middle.

Use a palette knife or spatula to carefully ease the hopper from the pan and lift it out. Serve the hoppers immediately, topped with the coconut or onion sambol and the kiri hodi, a wedge of lime and some fresh coriander. For those who like an extra kick, have chilli sauce ready to offer on the side. Repeat with the remaining batter, adding more oil to the pan as necessary, a teaspoon at a time. The hoppers can be reheated for 4–5 minutes in an oven preheated to 100°C/gas mark ¼ on a baking tray lined with greaseproof paper.

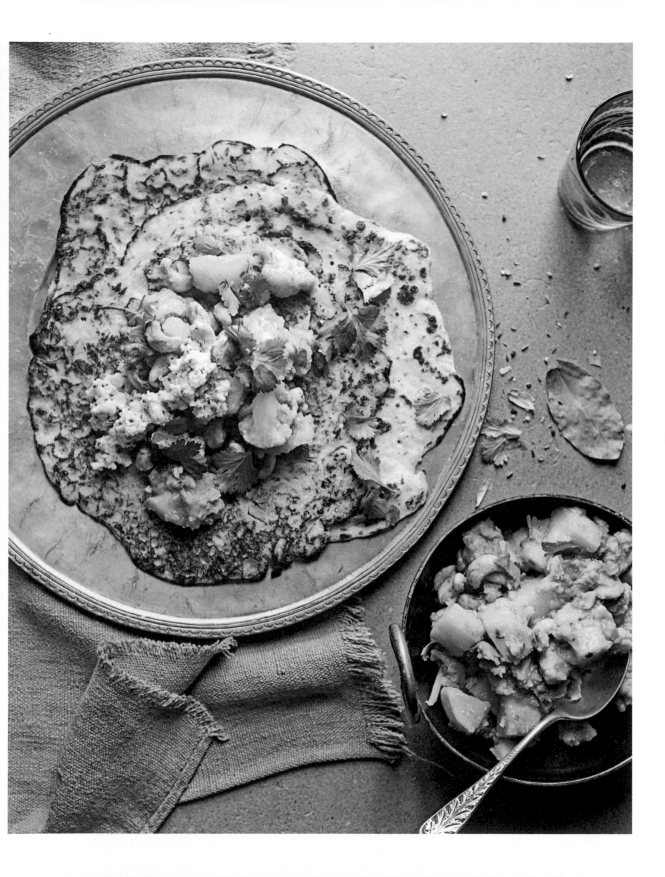

Chennai Dosa

POTATO, CAULIFLOWER AND CASHEW CURRY WITH COCONUT CHUTNEY

The dramatic crisp dosa I adore at the southern Indian restaurants in Tooting are quite a feat to pull off at home, because they need to be prepared over several days and require grinding and fermenting rice and *urad dhal* (black split peas). I like pancakes to be more of a spur-of-the-moment decision and I asked my friend, Romy Gill, chef-proprietor of Romy's Kitchen near Bristol, if she could suggest an easier alternative. This chennai dosa is her recipe with a few tweaks. It uses semolina flour, rice flour and buttermilk. It still takes practice to get the batter ultra-thin and crisp, although it is well worth persevering with. The potato, cauliflower and cashew curry is a family favourite adapted from a Sophie Grigson recipe and it makes this into a substantial meal. Simpler coconut potatoes would also make a good accompaniment. I adore fresh coconut chutney, although I admit that I cheated and used fresh coconut chunks rather than smashing my own coconut.

PREP

* plus 30 mins resting

COOK

TOTAL

DIETARY

USE GLUTEN-FREE
SELF-RAISING FLOUR

MAKES

8 x 24CM,
SERVES 4

125g semolina flour
125g rice flour, plus extra if needed
3 tablespoons self-raising flour
1 green chilli, deseeded and chopped
½ teaspoon dried chilli flakes
3cm piece of fresh ginger, peeled and grated
1 red onion, chopped
5 fresh curry leaves
a handful of coriander leaves, chopped
1 teaspoon cumin seeds, crushed
500ml buttermilk
sunflower oil or rapeseed oil, for cooking
salt and freshly ground black pepper

FOR THE POTATO, CAULIFLOWER
AND CASHEW CURRY
1 large onion, roughly chopped
2 garlic cloves, finely chopped
2.5cm piece of fresh ginger, peeled and grated
1 dried chilli, deseeded and chopped
1 teaspoon ground turmeric
1 tablespoon ground cumin
3 tablespoons sunflower oil or rapeseed oil
450g potatoes, peeled and cut into small cubes

½ cauliflower, broken into small florets
1 tablespoon lemon juice
100g shelled cashew nuts
3 tablespoons roughly chopped coriander leaves

FOR THE COCONUT CHUTNEY
1 tablespoon sunflower oil or rapeseed oil
1 teaspoon black mustard seeds
4 dried curry leaves
1 green chilli, deseeded and chopped
2cm piece of fresh ginger, peeled and chopped
zest and juice of 1 lime
100g fresh coconut, diced into small pieces

FOR THE GARAM MASALA
1 tablespoon cumin seeds
1 tablespoon coriander seeds
1 teaspoon fennel seeds
8 green cardamom pods
1 teaspoon black peppercorns
2 bay leaves
1 teaspoon ground cinnamon

Sift all the flours into a large bowl and add the green chilli and chilli flakes, ginger, onion, curry leaves, coriander leaves, cumin seeds and a little salt, then mix well. Gradually whisk in the buttermilk to make a thin batter without any lumps. Add 2 tablespoons water if it seems too thick, or if it seems too thin add a little more rice flour to thicken it. Rest for 30 minutes.

Meanwhile, to make the curry, put the onion into the smallest bowl of a food processor and add the garlic, ginger, chilli, turmeric, cumin, 1 teaspoon salt and 2 tablespoon water, then whizz to a paste. Heat 2 tablespoons sunflower oil in a wide, heavy-based saucepan over a medium heat and add the spice paste. Cook, stirring constantly, for 3 minutes.

Add the potatoes and cauliflower, and stir to coat with the paste, add 100ml water and the lemon juice, and bring to the boil. Reduce to a simmer over a low heat and cook, covered, for 10–15 minutes until the vegetables are tender but not collapsing. If there is still a lot of liquid, take the lid off and allow most of the water to cook off.

Meanwhile, put 1 tablespoon sunflower oil in a small frying pan over a medium–high heat and fry the cashews until lightly brown. Stir into the curry and cook for 1–2 minutes until blended.

To make the chutney, heat a small frying pan with the oil and fry the mustard seeds and curry leaves until they start to sizzle. Transfer to a blender and add the chilli, ginger, lime zest and juice, coconut and a little salt. Whizz, and add 100ml hot water, to make a thick paste.

To make the garam masala, put the cumin seeds in a small, heavy frying pan and add the coriander and fennel seeds, cardamom pods and black peppercorns. Heat over a low heat for 2–3 minutes until they begin to smell aromatic. Remove from the heat, cool a little, then add the bay leaves and cinnamon. Crush the mixture using a pestle and mortar. This will make more than you need, but it is a useful mix to have on stand-by. Set aside.

Preheat the oven to 100°C/gas mark ¼ and warm a plate to keep the dosas warm while you make them. Remove from the oven and turn off the oven. To cook the dosas, heat a non stick frying pan over a medium–high heat and add 1 tablespoon sunflower oil. Spread oil evenly with kitchen paper. Pour a ladleful of batter into the pan, and either immediately swirl it around so that the batter spreads out evenly and thinly or use a circular motion with a wooden crêpe spreader, spreading thinly from the centre to the edges.

Add 1 teaspoon of the oil on the top of the dosa to make it more crisp. Cook for 1–2 minutes making sure that the base is golden. Flip over and cook for 1–2 minutes until golden. Transfer the dosa to a warm plate. Keep warm with a clean tea-towel over the plate while cooking the remaining dosas. Repeat with the remaining batter, adding more oil to the pan as necessary.

Sprinkle the garam masala mix and the coriander leaves over the curry. Serve with the dosa and coconut chutney.

Okonomiyaki

PRAWNS, SPICY TAMARIND SAUCE AND JAPANESE MAYO

Okonomiyaki-ya restaurants are hugely popular in Japan, often offering the option to cook one's own over a teppan, a hotplate. The name means 'as you like it, grilled', so there really is not one defining recipe. They are made with *okonomiyaki* flour, dashi stock, eggs and an obligatory cabbage filling, plus whatever you have to hand, whether it is seafood, pork or bacon. The Japanese, however, are quite strict about their garnishes, which should include a special sweet-and-sour condiment rather like brown sauce, Japanese *kewpie* mayo, seaweed powder and bonito flakes that dance on the top of the hot *okonomiyaki* and impart plenty of umami richness. All are widely available at specialist Japanese stores. This recipe is *okonomiyaki* Osaka-style, where all the ingredients are mixed together rather than layered and served on top of fried noodles as in Hiroshima.

PREP 15 mins

COOK 10 mins

TOTAL 25 mins

DIETARY

USE A RICE-FLOUR-BASED OKONOMIYAKI FLOUR

MAKES

2 x 24CM
SERVES 2

200g okonomiyaki flour
200ml water or half water:half dashi
½ pointy hispi cabbage, finely shredded
4 spring onions, finely chopped
200g raw jumbo prawns, or thinly sliced pork belly, thinly sliced unsmoked bacon or tofu
3cm piece of fresh ginger, grated
50g tenkasu tempura batter balls (optional)

2 large eggs, beaten
groundnut oil, for cooking

TO SERVE
Japanese kewpie mayonnaise
okonomiyaki sauce, bought or homemade (see below)
2 tablespoons dried bonito flakes
2 tablespoons aonori seaweed
2 tablespoons pickled ginger

Preheat the oven to 100°C/gas mark ¼ and warm a plate to keep the *okonomiyaki* warm while you make them. In a large bowl, mix together the flour and 200ml water. Add the cabbage to the batter, then the spring onions, prawns, ginger and tenkasu balls, if using. Add the eggs and mix everything together gently.

Heat 1 tablespoon oil in a lidded frying pan over a medium heat. Pour in half the *okonomiyaki* mixture and flatten it with a spatula to form a round pancake about 1.5cm thick. Cook for 5 minutes or until golden, covering the pan with the lid to ensure it is evenly cooked. Flip over and cook, again covered, for a further 5 minutes. Keep warm. Repeat with the remaining mixture. Serve with mayo and *okonomiyaki* sauce drizzled over in ribbons and bonito flakes, aonori seaweed and pickled ginger scattered decorously.

To make *okonomiyaki* sauce, put 100ml dashi stock in a pan over a medium–high heat. Add 5 tablespoons Worcestershire sauce, 2 tablespoons tomato ketchup, 2 tablespoons tomato purée, 2 tablespoons tamarind paste, 2 tablespoons dark soy sauce, 2 tablespoons apple juice, 1 teaspoon brown sugar and 1 teaspoon honey. Bring to the boil, stirring well to prevent it catching on the base of the pan. Put 2 teaspoons cornflour in a bowl and stir in 3 teaspoons cold water. Add the cornflour mixture a little at a time to the hot mixture, stirring well. Cook over a low heat for 5 minutes or until the sauce has thickened to the consistency of a glossy ketchup. Leave to cool, then transfer to a jug. Store in the fridge until ready to use.

Banh Xeo

This is a crisp and lacy bright-yellow pancake from Vietnam that is far more substantial than a spring roll. Its name means 'sizzling cake' derived from the impressively loud sizzling sound the rice flour and coconut milk batter makes when it is dropped into the hot pan. *Bang xeo* is traditionally served with both pork and prawns, although I've made a lighter version with just prawns and added extra crisp vegetables. For a vegan version, add fine strips of mooli and carrots and leave out the prawns altogether. *Banh xeo* is immensely pleasing, with complex layers of flavour, texture and freshness. The distinction between a good and a brilliant *banh xeo* is in the thinness and crispness of the batter. I also like that it is usually eaten wrapped in lettuce leaves with masses of fragrant herbs.

PREP 25 mins

* plus 30 mins to overnight resting

COOK 10 mins

TOTAL 45 mins

DIETARY

BATTER IS GLUTEN-FREE AND VEGAN

MAKES

6 x 24CM, SERVES 3

200g brown rice flour
½ teaspoon salt
1 teaspoon ground turmeric
300ml coconut milk
150ml warm water
3 tablespoons groundnut oil, or sunflower oil or rapeseed oil, for cooking

FOR THE DIPPING SAUCE
40ml lime juice
1½ tablespoons sesame oil
1 tablespoon brown sugar
1 tablespoon rice wine vinegar
1 tablespoon sweet soy sauce (kecap manis)
2cm piece of fresh ginger, peeled and grated
1 small Thai red chilli, or to taste, finely chopped

1 garlic clove, crushed
½ teaspoon salt
50ml warm water

FOR THE FILLING
3 tablespoons groundnut oil, or sunflower oil or rapeseed oil
1 onion, finely sliced
100g shitake mushrooms, finely sliced
150g mangetouts, sliced into thin strips
150g raw prawns
150g beansprouts
3 spring onions, diagonally sliced

TO SERVE
1 Romaine lettuce
15g coriander leaves
15g mint leaves
15g Thai basil leaves

Preheat the oven to 100°C/gas mark ¼ and warm a plate to keep the pancakes warm while you make them. Put the rice flour in a bowl and add the salt and turmeric. Slowly pour in the coconut milk, whisking to ensure there are no lumps, until you have a batter the consistency of single cream. Add up to 150ml warm water to thin the batter, if necessary. Set aside to rest for at least 30 minutes or overnight.

To make the dipping sauce, put all the ingredients in a bowl with 50ml warm water and whisk together, ensuring the sugar is dissolved. Set aside.

To make the filling, heat 2 tablespoons of the oil in a large frying pan, add the onion and mushrooms, and cook gently until the onion softens and the mushrooms start to brown. Add the mangetouts and stir to warm through but to retain their crispness. Remove from the pan. Heat the remaining oil in the frying pan over a medium heat. Add the prawns and cook for 1–2 minutes until pink, then stir in the mushroom mixture. Keep warm with a lid over a very low heat.

To cook the pancakes, heat a large, heavy frying pan over a medium heat and add 1 tablespoon oil. Spread evenly with kitchen paper so that the oil covers the base very lightly. Turn the heat up to high and, when the oil is very hot, pour in 4 tablespoons of the batter, and immediately swirl it around so that the batter spreads out to the edges of the pan. The edges can be thinner than the centre of the *banh xeo* to encourage them to crisp.

Add a small handful of the mushroom mixture, with some beansprouts and spring onion. Cover the pan with a lid and cook for 3 minutes or until the *banh xeo* turns very crisp. It should be golden at the edges and coming away from the pan. Remove the lid and use a spatula to fold one half of the pancake over the other. Transfer to the warmed plate and keep warm in the oven. Repeat the process until you have six pancakes – the batter may need to be re-whisked after each *banh xeo* to ensure there are no lumps.

Serve the *banh xeo* with plenty of lettuce leaves, coriander, mint and Thai basil with the dipping sauce in small bowls on the side. The traditional way to eat *banh xeo* is to take a lettuce leaf, pile some herbs onto it, then break off a piece of the pancake and place it inside the leaf. Roll it up like a spring roll and dip it into the sauce.

Galettes de Sarrasin

LEEKS, MERGUEZ SAUSAGE AND HARISSA YOGURT

Brittany is home to savoury crêpes made with buckwheat flour called galettes de sarrasin. I remember many a Breton childhood holiday full of galettes. My favourite was always the galette complet, with a whole egg cracked into the galette plus some spinach and folded in on itself like an envelope. Buckwheat flour is easy to find now. I usually make half and half with plain flour, however, as buckwheat alone can taste rather dense, although I do like its nutty, toasty flavour. Bretons often add a splash of beer to the batter. Traditionally, the first galette is a disaster and either discarded or cut up and put into soup, so don't be disheartened.
Aside from the classics, including ham and Gruyère, which is satisfyingly gooey, I like something punchy, such as caramelised leeks with grilled merguez sausages and a good dollop of yogurt with harissa. The galettes can be prepared with sweet fillings too. A classic is apples and salted caramel sauce.

PREP

* plus 2 hours or overnight resting

COOK

TOTAL

DIETARY

USE GLUTEN-FREE
FLOUR AND SOYA MILK
OR ALMOND MILK

MAKES

8 x 24CM (BEFORE
FOLDING),
SERVES 4

200g buckwheat flour
50g plain flour
½ teaspoon fine sea salt
2 large eggs
500ml semi-skimmed milk
2 tablespoons rose harissa
a handful of fresh mint leaves, torn
200g Greek yogurt
8 merguez sausages

sunflower oil or rapeseed oil, for
cooking
green salad, to serve

FOR THE CARAMALIZED LEEKS
2 tablespoon extra virgin olive oil
30g butter
4 leeks, cut into 5cm pieces
2 tablespoon soft brown sugar

Sift the flours and salt into a large mixing bowl and make a little well in the centre. Break the eggs into the well, and whisk them gradually into the flour in a circular motion.

Pour the milk in slowly, whisking all the time. Add 500ml of cold water, still whisking. Cover and put in the fridge for at least 2 hours, or ideally overnight.

Meanwhile, to make the caramelised leeks, heat the oil and butter in a pan, add the leeks and cook for 10 minutes to wilt, then add the sugar. Add enough water to cover and cook for 10 minutes or until the water has evaporated. Set aside.

Stir the rose harissa and mint leaves into the yogurt, then set aside.

Take the batter out of the fridge and re-whisk, as some of the flour will have settled at the base of the bowl. Preheat the grill and cook the merguez for 10–15 minutes or until cooked through. Keep warm.

Preheat the oven to 100°C/gas mark ¼ and put a large baking tray in the oven to keep the galettes warm while you make them.

Heat a large frying pan over a high heat. When very hot, smear on sunflower oil using kitchen paper to leave a shimmer of oil on the pan. Pour a ladleful of batter into the pan, and immediately swirl it around so that the batter spreads out into an even circle. Reduce the heat to medium and cook for 2 minutes or until golden underneath. Flip over and cook for a further 2 minutes or until golden.

Put the caramelised leek, and merguez, chopped into chunks, in the middle of the galette. Fold the galette: the traditional way is to fold in the four sides to make a square parcel. If there is lots of filling, just fold two sides in.

Keep the filled galettes warm in the baking tray in the oven and repeat with the remaining batter, adding more oil to the pan as necessary. Serve with harissa yogurt and accompany with a green salad and, preferably, generous amounts of Breton sparkling cider.

Cornmeal Chorizo Pancakes

CABRALES BLUE CHEESE SAUCE, TOMATO AND LIME SALSA

Asturias is an astoundingly dramatic, green and wild region of Spain, which is still, inexplicably, little touched by tourism. I remember having a similar cornmeal pancake to this on the wooden veranda of a village café with stunning views of the Picos de Europa mountains. The pancake is light yet rich with a grainy sweetness from the cornmeal, and the chorizo adds a spicy note and a chewy texture. Cabrales is an exceptionally strong artisan blue cheese produced only in Asturias and available at specialist Spanish stores (or you can substitute Gorgonzola), giving this dish serious punch. It has to be experienced. The fresh tomato salsa adds a refreshing antidote.

PREP 20 mins

COOK 15 mins

TOTAL 35 mins

DIETARY

USE GLUTEN-FREE CORNMEAL

MAKES

12 x 10CM, SERVES 4

170ml soured cream
1 large egg
120g cornmeal or maize meal
60g plain flour
1 teaspoon baking powder
½ teaspoon bicarbonate of soda
pinch of salt
200g cooked chorizo, finely chopped
4 tablespoon finely chopped parsley
olive oil, for cooking

FOR THE TOMATO AND LIME SALSA
250g cherry tomatoes, quartered
zest of 1 lime and juice of ½ lime

FOR THE CABRALES SAUCE
170g single cream
200g cabrales or gorgonzola cheese, chopped

sea salt and freshly ground black pepper

Preheat the oven to 100°C/gas mark ¼ and warm a plate for the pancakes.

To make the tomato and lime salsa, stir all the ingredients together in a bowl. Set aside.

Whisk together the soured cream and egg in a medium bowl using an electric or hand whisk. Put the cornmeal in a large bowl and sift in the flour, baking powder, bicarbonate of soda and salt. Mix together using a wooden spoon. Stir in the soured cream mixture thoroughly to ensure there are no lumps. Add the chorizo and parsley, and a good grinding of pepper.

Heat a large, non-stick frying pan over a medium–high heat, then add 1 tablespoon oil and spread it thinly over the pan using kitchen paper. Add 2 tablespoons of batter to make each pancake about 10cm in size and flatten the batter quickly. Cook for 2–3 minutes or until golden. Flip over and cook for a further 1–2 minutes. Keep warm in the oven. Repeat with the remaining batter, adding more oil to the pan as necessary.

Meanwhile, heat the cream in a pan over a medium heat, add the cabrales and allow it to melt slowly. Season with pepper to taste. There is no need to add salt as the cheese is quite salty.

To serve, pour the cabrales sauce over the chorizo pancakes and put the tomato and lime salsa on the side.

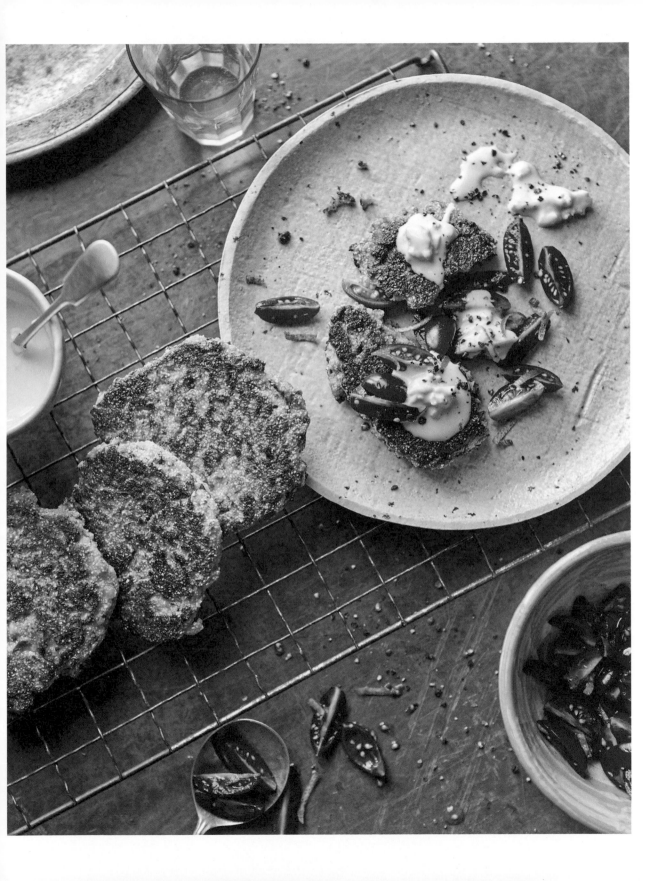

Jian Bing

Vendors are found in every neighbourhood in China selling *jian bing* – one of China's favourite street breakfasts. It's long been a well-kept culinary secret. I've only recently come across self-taught Western pioneers bringing *jian bing* to America and Europe. Mee Mee Street Cart, owned by twins Melissa and Oliver Fu, who pop up in London and Manchester, produce the best I've ever tasted, so I was determined to make a version at home with the help of my Singaporean friend, Loretta Liu, chef-owner of Café On in London. What makes crisp-fried *jian bing* pancakes so appealing is the bold yin-and-yang contrasts of flavour and texture. It's like a firework of taste: the soft egg spread across the crêpe-thin pancake (made with millet flour though traditionally mung bean flour is used) as it cooks; the puffy, crackly wonton skins; the zingy freshness of coriander, cucumber, iceberg lettuce and crunchy spring onions; and the sweet-spicy-salty hit of hoisin and chilli sauce. I decided to add Chinese five-spice duck as a nod to the Peking duck I so relish, making the *jian bing* substantial enough for a meal.

Jian bing have a longer history than almost any other Chinese street food. I'm intrigued by the legend that suggests they originated in Shandong Province during the Three Kingdoms Period (AD220–80), when military strategist, Zhuge Liang, had his soldiers cook batter on shields held over the fire after their woks were lost!

PREP 20 mins

COOK 45 mins

TOTAL 65 mins

DIETARY

USE GLUTEN FREE FLOUR, SOYA MILK

MAKES

4 X 24CM (BEFORE FOLDING), SERVES 4

2 duck breasts
2 tablespoons Chinese five-spice powder
1 tablespoon sunflower oil or rapeseed oil, plus extra for shallow frying
210g jar of good hoisin sauce or yellow bean paste
8 tablespoons sriracha chilli sauce
8 wonton wrappers
4 large eggs
a large bunch of spring onions, diagonally chopped

½ cucumber, peeled and cut into small sticks
½ iceberg lettuce, finely chopped
a large bunch of coriander, leaves finely chopped

FOR THE BATTER
220g millet flour or plain flour, or a mixture of both
120ml milk or soya milk
sunflower oil or rapeseed oil, for cooking

Preheat the oven to 180°C/gas mark 8. Set a rack over a roasting tin. Pat the duck breasts dry with kitchen paper. Score the skin with a knife, then rub with the five-spice powder.

Put the duck skin-side down in a cold, heavy frying pan, then turn the heat to medium–high add the oil and cook for 6–8 minutes until crisp, pouring off the fat regularly. Seal the other side for 30 seconds. Put skin-side up on the prepared roasting tin and cook for 10 minutes for rare or 15 minutes for medium. Leave to rest in a warm place for 10 minutes. Slice thinly.

Meanwhile, to make the batter, put the millet in a bowl and add the milk and 120ml water. Use an electric whisk to make a thin batter the consistency of whipping cream. Add a further splash of water, if necessary, to thin it.

In a separate bowl, mix the hoisin sauce and chilli sauce. Slice the wonton wrappers into thin strips. Heat a deep heavy frying pan or wok with sunflower oil to a depth of 3cm and heat until very hot, about 175°C (test by dropping in one slice of wonton; it should bubble straight away). Fry the wonton strips in batches for 2–3 minutes until lightly golden and crisp, spreading them out in the pan so that they don't stick. Remove with a slotted spoon and drain on kitchen paper.

Heat a large, heavy non-stick frying pan over a medium heat. Add 1 tablespoon oil. Ladle a quarter of the batter into the pan, and either immediately swirl it around so that the batter spreads out to cover the entire pan or spread it evenly with a spatula. Cook for 1–2 minutes until golden on the base yet still white on the top and just beginning to firm up.

Show bravado and crack one whole egg straight onto the jian bing (as the street vendors would do) or beat 1 egg and pour it over the jian bing, then spread it evenly. Cook for 2 minutes or until the egg is just set. Flip over and cook the egg side for up to 30 seconds or until lightly golden. Flip back so that the egg side is on top.

On one half of the pancake add some spring onion slices, cucumber sticks, iceberg lettuce and 1 tablespoon chopped coriander, then press firmly into the egg. On the other half, spread 3 tablespoons hoisin and chilli sauce mix and top with slices of duck. Add crisp wonton strips on top of the duck and vegetables.

Flip the top third of the pancake down over the wonton strips and flip the base third of the pancake up, then fold it in half. Fold kitchen paper in half and use it to hold the *jian bing*. Serve immediately. Repeat with the remaining batter, adding more oil to the pan as necessary.

Panqueta

WITH SPICED BEEF, OLIVES, TOMATO AND CHIMICHURRI

For a really hearty, meaty pancake, the Brazilians – who love their beef – have a truly comforting pancake dish based on minced beef, tomato and olives that I have given extra punch with *chimichurri*. It is the sort of pancake I make when I need a metaphorical warm hug.

PREP 30 mins

COOK 40 mins

TOTAL 70 mins

DIETARY

USE GLUTEN-FREE FLOUR

MAKES

6 X 24CM, SERVES 4

120g plain flour, sifted
1 egg and 1 yolk, beaten
250ml semi-skimmed milk
3 tablespoons chopped oregano leaves
butter, for greasing
sea salt and freshly ground black pepper
sunflower or rapeseed oil
green salad with bitter leaves, to serve

FOR THE CHIMICHURRI
1 large bunch of flat-leaf parsley, leaves finely chopped
1 bunch coriander, leaves finely chopped
2 garlic cloves, crushed
1 jalapeño chilli, deseeded and chopped
5 tablespoons red wine vinegar
juice of 1 lemon
5 tablespoons extra virgin olive oil

FOR THE BEEF AND TOMATO FILLING
2 tablespoons sunflower or rapeseed oil
2 red onions, finely chopped
2 garlic cloves, crushed
1 green chilli, deseeded and finely chopped
1 teaspoon ground cumin
1 teaspoon ground coriander
450g minced beef
400g passata or chopped tomatoes
2 tablespoons tomato purée
2 tablespoons balsamic vinegar
50g pitted green olives, chopped
3 tablespoons chopped parsley leaves
30g Parmesan, grated

To make the chimichurri, put all the ingredients in a bowl and mix them together, add sea salt to taste and then leave it to macerate for 3 hours.

Grease a large ovenproof dish and set aside. Put the flour in a large bowl. Make a well in the centre and add the beaten eggs. Gradually whisk in the milk using an electric or hand whisk to form a smooth batter the consistency of single cream. Stir in the chopped oregano and season to taste. Leave the batter to rest for at least 30 minutes before cooking.

Preheat the oven to 100°C/gas mark ¼ and heat a plate to keep the pancakes warm while you make them.

Meanwhile, to make the beef filling, heat the oil in a large saucepan. Add the onions and cook for 5 minutes or until soft and lightly golden. Stir in the garlic, chilli, cumin and coriander, and cook for 3 minutes. Add the beef and stir well so that it browns thoroughly. Add the passata, tomato purée and balsamic vinegar. Bring to the boil, then reduce the heat and simmer uncovered for 30 minutes. Add the olives and parsley, and season with salt and pepper.

To make the pancakes, place a large non-stick crêpe pan over a medium heat. Add a tablespoon of oil and tilt the pan to cover the base completely. When properly hot, pour in 1 ladleful of batter and cook for 1 minute or until just set and golden underneath. Flip over and cook for 30 seconds or until lightly golden. Put the pancakes on the warmed plate, interleaved with greaseproof paper. Repeat with the remaining batter, adding more oil to the pan as necessary. The batter should make at least eight pancakes.

Increase the oven temperature to 200°C/gas mark 6 and remove the warm pancakes from the oven. Pour a line of beef sauce across the lower bottom half of one pancake and fold the lower edge over the sauce to cover it. Roll up neatly and put in the buttered ovenproof dish. Repeat with remaining pancakes, arranging them in a single layer.

Top the pancakes with grated Parmesan, then bake for 10 minutes or until the cheese is bubbling and brown. Serve with plenty of chimichurri drizzled over the top, and a big green salad made with mustardy/bitter leaves.

Teatime & Desserts

Aebleskiver

These utterly moreish pancakes are like crisp, light, fluffy doughnuts. They are traditionally eaten at Christmas in Denmark and served with mulled wine. To make them, you need a cast-iron *æbleskiver* pan that has five or seven spherical indentations. They are not expensive and are relatively easy to come by. Before using for the first time, the pan needs to be seasoned by oiling it all over and heating it in an extremely hot oven until nearly smoking for about 1 hour, then wiping off the excess oil. Mastering the art of turning an *æbleskiver* takes time, especially following the Danish tradition of using 2 knitting needles to do it! (I used wooden skewers instead.) It does take a certain amount of courage and belief to turn them while they are still soft but, believe me, the four quarter-turns I explain below are essential and the technique does work. Take care not to have the heat too high.

PREP 20 mins

COOK 20 mins

TOTAL 40 mins

DIETARY

USE GLUTEN-FREE PLAIN FLOUR

MAKES

16 x 5CM, SERVES 4

2 large egg whites
50g icing sugar, sifted
1 teaspoon ground cinnamon
250g plain flour
2 tablespoons golden caster sugar
½ teaspoon bicarbonate of soda
½ teaspoon salt

2 large egg yolks
475ml buttermilk
60g butter, melted
200ml sunflower oil or rapeseed oil, for cooking
wild blueberry jam and whipped cream, to serve

Preheat the oven to 100°C/gas mark ¼ and put in a rack on a baking tray to keep the *æbleskiver* warm while you make them.

Put the egg whites in a clean, grease-free bowl and whisk until they form stiff peaks. Combine the icing sugar and cinnamon in a bowl for sprinkling later.

In another bowl, mix the flour, sugar, bicarbonate of soda, salt, egg yolks, buttermilk and melted butter. Carefully fold in the whisked egg whites. Make the *æbleskiver* immediately.

Place the *æbleskiver* pan over a medium heat for a few minutes until it is really hot. Put 6 tablespoons sunflower oil in a small bowl. Using a heatproof pastry brush, liberally oil the base of each indentation. Pour about 2 tablespoons batter into each hole, filling it about three-quarters full. The batter should sizzle as it goes in. Cook for 1–2 minutes until the *æbleskiver* start to bubble on the surface and look as if they are starting to set around the edges. Immediately, turn a quarter-turn using a wooden skewer, a chopstick or a fork. The technique is to slide the skewer between the edge of the pan and the cooked edge of the puffed pancake, then to move it so that it turns and the cooked part is lifted out of the pan. The uncooked batter will run into the base of the pan. Continue cooking a bit more, twisting the *æbleskiver* three further quarter-turns to form a puffy ball shape, allowing 1–2 minutes to cook each turn to a light golden colour, and ensuring they don't burn. Repeat with the remaining batter, brushing each hole with a little more oil before cooking the next batch. Serve the *æbleskiver* rolled in the cinnamon sugar with blueberry jam and whipped cream.

Fluffy Coconut Pancakes

WITH THYME-BAKED APRICOTS

Coconut flour is delectable in pancakes, yet quite a challenge to work with. It is extraordinarily absorbent of liquids and requires more eggs and buttermilk than seems imaginable to form a batter that is not too porridge-like and crumbly and which will hold together properly when cooking. It is worth persevering, as it gives a beautiful sweetly fragrant flavour and a wonderful fluffy texture to pancakes. What's more, coconut flour, made from the pressed coconut 'meat', is very high in protein and fibre, and extremely filling. I first came across coconut flour when visiting Canada to see how maple trees are tapped to produce maple syrup. Baked maple apricots make a lovely accompaniment, although fresh nectarines work superbly in summer too.

PREP 20 mins

COOK 30 mins

TOTAL 50 mins

DIETARY

COCONUT FLOUR IS
GLUTEN-FREE

MAKES

12 x 10CM,
SERVES 4

4 large eggs
2 tablespoons coconut oil, melted
1 tablespoon honey
1 teaspoon vanilla extract
100ml coconut milk
200ml buttermilk
75g coconut flour
2 teaspoons baking powder
1 teaspoon bicarbonate of soda
¼ teaspoon salt
30g butter, for cooking

FOR THE APRICOTS
12 apricots, halved and pitted
zest of 1 lemon and juice of ½ lemon
6 sprigs of thyme
1 vanilla pod, broken in half
3 tablespoons Canadian maple syrup,
plus extra to serve
1 teaspoon vanilla extract

Preheat the oven to 180°C/gas mark 4 and butter a large baking dish.

To make the apricots, put them cut-side up in the prepared dish. Sprinkle over the lemon zest and juice, add 2 tablespoons water and tuck in the thyme and vanilla pod. Mix the maple syrup with the vanilla extract and drizzle over the apricots. Bake for 15–20 minutes until tender. Remove from the oven and turn the oven off. Put a plate in the oven to keep the pancakes warm while you make them.

Meanwhile, put the eggs in a bowl and add the coconut oil, honey and vanilla extract. Mix together well. Stir in the coconut milk and buttermilk. In another bowl, mix together the coconut flour, baking powder, bicarbonate of soda and salt. Add the egg mixture to the dry ingredients, stirring gently. The batter will be thick and fluffy.

Melt a little butter in a large non-stick heavy frying pan over a medium heat. Add 2 tablespoons of batter for each pancake and flatten slightly. Cook as many pancakes as will fit at one time. Cook for 2 minutes or until the underneath is lightly golden, check by using a spatula, as the batter won't bubble. Flip over carefully and cook for a further 1–2 minutes until golden. Keep the pancakes warm, and repeat with the remaining batter, adding more butter to the pan as necessary. Serve warm with the apricots and extra maple syrup for added indulgence.

Pannukakku Finnish Pancake

An unusual pancake with real wow factor, this Finnish *pannukakku* is baked in the oven and puffs up as dramatically as a soufflé. It has a delectable custardy interior and a crisp crust and is in essence rather like a French clafoutis. Traditionally, it is served with a rhubarb and strawberry compote, providing an excitingly different flavour combination that mixes tart and sweet. The compote works brilliantly with the pancake, which must be served at once. Although the compote is usually served cold, I find it is just as scrumptious warm. This pancake is really easy to knock up and is an impressive addition to a dinner party.

PREP 20 mins
* plus 1 hour resting

COOK 20 mins

TOTAL 40 mins

DIETARY

USE GLUTEN-FREE
PLAIN FLOUR

MAKES

1 x 28CM,
SERVES 4, OR 2 GREEDY
PEOPLE!

50g butter, melted
120g plain flour, sifted
½ teaspoon vanilla extract
2 tablespoons clear honey
2 large eggs, beaten
300ml semi-skimmed milk

FOR THE COMPOTE
500g rhubarb, cut into 3cm pieces
zest and juice of 1 orange

60g soft brown sugar
200g strawberries, finely sliced

FOR THE VANILLA CRÈME FRAÎCHE
1 tablespoon vanilla sugar or 1
teaspoon icing sugar and ½ teaspoon
vanilla extract
200ml crème fraîche

Preheat the oven to 220°C/gas mark 7. Put a 20cm ovenproof cast-iron frying pan or baking dish in the oven to heat up.

Put 40g of the melted butter in a large bowl and add the flour, vanilla, honey, eggs and milk. Mix together using a hand whisk to make a pouring batter with the consistency of double cream. Leave to stand for 1 hour, as this will make it rise better.

Use the remaining melted butter to coat the heated frying pan, brushing it up the sides. Pour in the batter and put the pan in the hot oven. Cook for 20–25 minutes until the batter has dramatically risen, is a little crusty and golden brown at the edges, and looks like a just-set custard in the middle.

Meanwhile, make the compote. Put the rhubarb in a saucepan over a medium heat and add the orange juice and soft brown sugar. Cover the pan. Cook to dissolve the sugar and then bring to the boil. Reduce the heat to low and add the orange zest, then simmer for 6 minutes. Stir gently, then add the strawberries and cook for 2 minutes. The compote can be served warm or cold.

In a small bowl, stir the vanilla sugar, or icing sugar and vanilla extract mixture, into the crème fraîche. Serve the pancake immediately with the compote and vanilla crème fraîche.

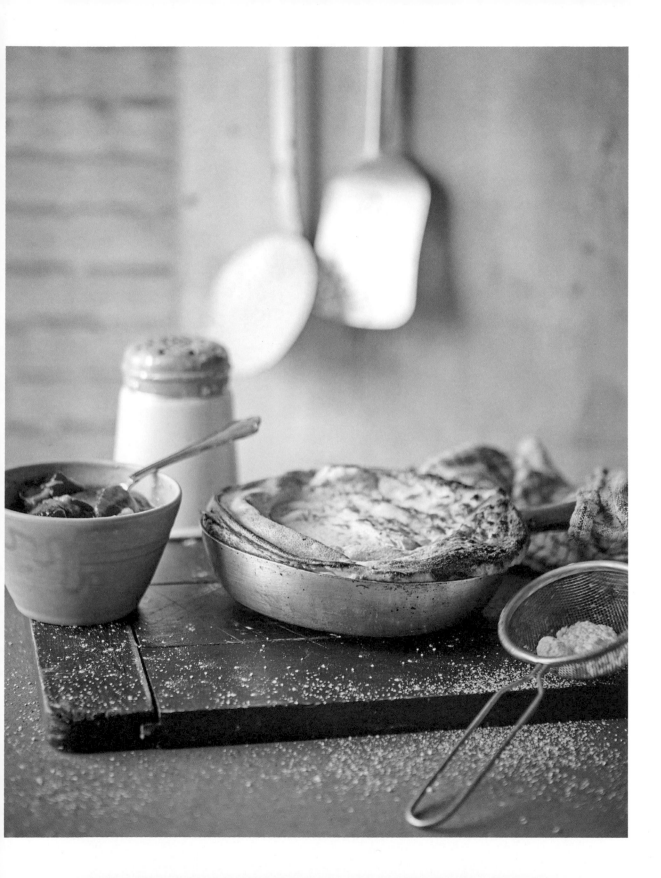

Blintzes

With a history dating back to at least the 1800s, *blintzes* are an essential dish in Ashkenazi Jewish homes throughout Central Europe. The name itself is Yiddish and means 'filled pancakes'. They are invariably served at Shavuot, an important Jewish festival that marks the giving of the Torah on Mount Sinai and the beginning of the wheat harvest. It is a time when eating dairy is encouraged.

I like *blintzes* all year round as a wonderfully comforting food for breakfast or a delectable dessert. What I particularly relish about these unusually soft crêpes is that their filling reminds me of baked cheesecake. No wonder they are so popular in New York!

I use a mixture of ricotta and cottage cheese for my filling, together with egg yolk, lemon zest and vanilla for a lighter touch, although traditionally it is a mixture of curd and cream cheese.

I have fond memories of my Hungarian great-grandmother baking a tray of *blintzes* when we visited her at her cosy, antimacassar-filled flat in west London. Doilies were de rigueur. Her blintzes were always finished with icing sugar and cinnamon, as cookery writer Claudia Roden suggests. It might seem counter-intuitive, but the crêpes are only cooked on one side initially, then, when they are baked or fried, the other side will brown beautifully. Blintzes are customarily served with apple sauce, although in the summer, a fresh cherry sauce, as used here, makes a delicious alternative.

PREP 20 mins

* plus 40 mins resting

COOK 30 mins

TOTAL 50 mins

DIETARY

USE GLUTEN-FREE PLAIN FLOUR

MAKES

8–10 x 24CM (BEFORE FILLING), SERVES 4

240g plain flour, sifted
240ml sparkling water
4 large eggs, beaten
50g butter, melted
pinch of salt
50ml boiling water
50g butter, cubed, plus extra for greasing
20g icing sugar, sifted
½ teaspoon ground cinnamon

FOR THE FILLING
250g ricotta
250g plain cottage cheese, drained

1 teaspoon vanilla extract
1 large egg yolk
50g icing sugar
zest of 1 lemon

FOR THE CHERRY SAUCE
400g fresh cherries, halved and pitted
zest and juice of 2 oranges
3 tablespoons golden caster sugar
1 teaspoon ground cinnamon
3 tablespoons dark rum

In a large bowl, whisk together the flour and sparkling water. Add the eggs, butter and salt. Whisk again until fully incorporated. The batter should have the consistency of double cream. Leave to rest for at least 10 minutes.

Meanwhile, to make the filling, put the cheeses in a large bowl or in a food processor and add the vanilla extract, egg yolk and icing sugar. Mix together, then put in the fridge for 30 minutes to firm up.

To make the cherry sauce, put the pitted cherries in a small pan with the orange zest and juice, sugar, cinnamon and rum. Heat gently to dissolve the sugar. Keep the sauce warm.

Before cooking the crêpes, add 50ml boiling water to the batter and whisk thoroughly. This ensures the *blintzes* are soft and pliable when rolling (it's a tip I picked up from Michael Zee of Symmetry Breakfast).

You can bake or fry your *blintzes* to finish them, though I prefer them baked. If baking, preheat the oven to 180°C/gas mark 4 and butter a baking dish. Preheat a non-stick frying pan. Test that it is hot enough by putting a few drops of water in the pan. If the water sizzles, it is perfect for cooking the crêpes. If bubbles burst, reduce the heat a little. Wipe the pan with a buttered piece of kitchen paper, then pour in sufficient batter to coat the pan thinly. Cook over a medium heat until the blintz is a little crispy around the edges and firm on top. Do not flip. Stack on a plate interleaved with kitchen paper. Repeat with the remaining batter, adding more butter to the pan each time. (This can be done ahead of assembling the next stage, if you like.)

When ready to serve fill the *blintzes*. Put a *blintz* on a flat surface cooked-side up. Put 2–3 tablespoons of cheese filling in the lower third of the *blintz* and flatten with the base of a spoon. Be sure not to overfill. Fold the base of the *blintz* over the filling and then fold the two sides into the middle and roll the *blintz* from the base to the top.

Put all the rolled blintz in the prepared baking dish. Scatter with cubes of butter. Bake for 15 minutes or until enticingly brown. Alternatively, the assembled *blintzes* can be fried in a large frying pan in melted butter for 4-5 minutes until crisp and golden, turning once .

Mix the icing sugar with the cinnamon and use to dust the cooked *blintzes*. Serve immediately with the warm cherry sauce. Traditionally, soured cream is served too, but I think this is probably over-gilding the *blintzes* which are plenty rich enough.

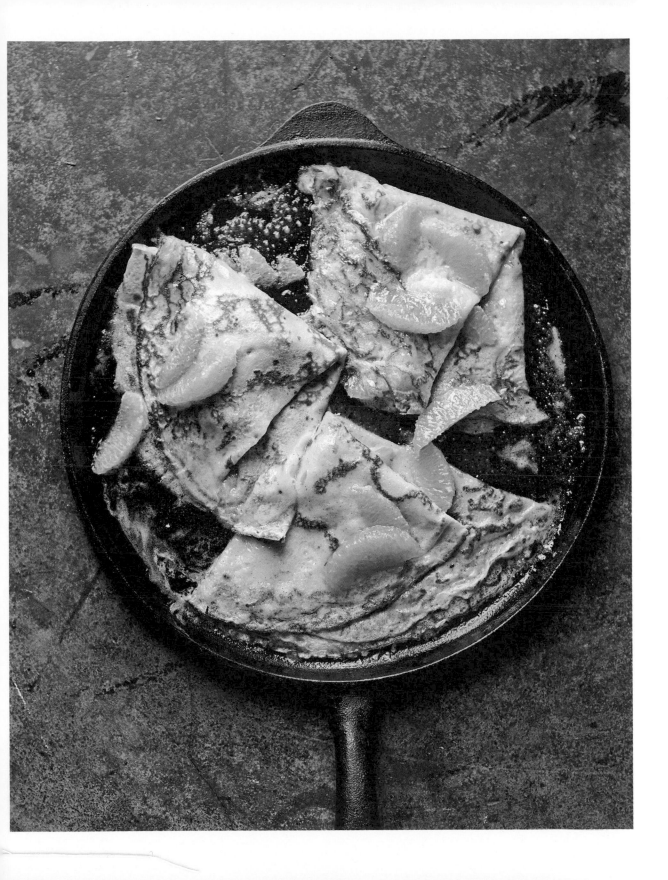

Crêpes Suzette

A timeless decadent dessert, crêpes Suzette always creates theatre when served. The first time I had them dished up with all due pomp and ceremony was at a dinner dance at The Ritz where they have been serving the dessert since 1906. It is wonderful to behold: an elegant trolley wheeled to the table and the crêpes impeccably made by waiters with white gloves. They certainly know how to flambé!

To modernise the dish, I've made a Suzette butter using a touch of yuzu juice for added zing.

The history of Crêpes Suzette allegedly dates back to an endearing accident in 1895, although Larousse Gastronomique disputes this story. Edward, Prince of Wales – the son of Queen Victoria and the future King Edward VII – was entertaining some gentleman friends and one of their French daughters at the Café de Paris in Monte Carlo. They ordered pancakes for dessert, which were pre-prepared in the kitchen and the orange sauce with liqueur finished at the table by a young waiter called Henri Charpentier (who went on to become a revered chef). The chafing dish accidently caught fire, but the flambé accident made the dish taste even better. Edward asked for the dish to be named after Suzette, his friend's young daughter.

I recently tried a rather different flambéed crêpe served with roast pineapple in a caramel sauce with pomegranate seeds, mint and rum at 45 Jermyn Street. This was also served at the table with all due ceremony cooked on a bespoke walnut-wood crêpe-making trolley.

PREP 30 mins
plus 1 hour resting

COOK 15 mins

TOTAL 45 mins

DIETARY

USE GLUTEN-FREE FLOUR, USE ALMOND OR SOYA MILK

MAKES

12 x 24CM, SERVES 4–6

175g plain flour, sifted
3 tablespoons sugar
zest of 1 orange
seeds from 1 vanilla pod
pinch of salt
500ml full-fat milk, or soya milk or almond milk
3 large eggs
80g butter, melted, plus extra for cooking
5 tablespoons Grand Marnier or Cointreau
4 blood oranges or other oranges

FOR THE SUZETTE BUTTER
110g golden caster sugar
zest of ½ orange and ½ lime
3 tablespoons yuzu or lime juice
150g butter, softened
1 tablespoons Grand Marnier or Cointreau

Put the flour in a large bowl and add the sugar, orange zest, vanilla seeds and salt. Combine well, then make a well in the centre.

In a separate bowl whisk the milk, eggs and melted butter. Gradually add to the flour mixture, whisking until very smooth. Whisk in the liqueur, then transfer the batter to a jug. Cover and set aside at room temperature to rest for 1 hour.

Meanwhile, make the Suzette butter. Put the sugar in a bowl and add the orange and lime zests and the yuzu juice. Stir to dissolve the sugar, then beat in the butter and stir in the liqueur. Set aside.

For the oragne slices, use a sharp knife to cut a thin slice of peel and pith from each end of an orange. Put cut-side down on a plate and cut off the rest of the peel and pith. Remove any remaining pith. Cut the flesh into slices, then repeat with the other oranges. Set aside.

Heat a crêpe pan over a medium–high heat and, using a heatproof pastry brush, brush with melted butter, then pour in enough batter to evenly yet thinly cover the base of the pan. Cook for 1–2 minutes until lightly golden underneath and bubbles appear on the surface. Flip over and cook for 1 minute. Wipe out the pan with kitchen paper and repeat with the remaining batter, adding more butter to the pan as before. Stack the crêpes as they cook and cover with foil.

To serve, fold the crêpes into quarters. Melt a third of the Suzette butter in a large frying pan over a medium heat, then add as many folded crêpes as will fit in the pan. Cook for 30 seconds to coat and reheat, then transfer the crêpes to a warmed flameproof dish. Add the orange slices. Repeat with the remaining crêpes, adding a little more Suzette butter each time. Add any remaining Suzette butter to the pan, bring to a simmer and cook to a syrup consistency, then pour a little more over the crêpes and put any remaining butter in a jug to serve alongside the crêpes.

Return the pan to the heat and add the liqueur to heat. Carefully ignite with a long match, tilting the pan away from you. Be warned, the alcohol should burst into flames. Pour the flaming liqueur over the crêpes. Serve them warm with the orange slices and any remaining Suzette butter to pour over.

Lemon Crunch Pancakes

Everyone enjoys pancakes on Shrove Tuesday, when they're traditionally eaten to use up all the fat before Lent. In fact, a straw poll of friends suggested that pancakes with the classic lemon and sugar topping remains a top favourite. I will often put melted butter in my pancake batter, making it, strictly speaking, a crêpe mix, but in this instance I prefer to keep my pancakes plainer and crisper and merely cook them in butter. Somehow it makes a better foil for all the tart lemon juice and crunchy sugar (granulated is a must). Although do experiment with coconut sugar if you can get some, as it adds a delectable, rich note. Adding an extra egg yolk to the batter is also good for enhancing its flavour. Even if you don't usually rest your batter, a mere 30 minutes makes a difference, as it helps the starch in the flour to absorb the liquid and allows the air bubbles from whisking to disperse. I cook my pancakes over a fairly brisk heat, because I like them as thin and crisp as possible with lacy edges, although turn the heat lower if you want a softer paler 'French' finish. If you're selflessly making a batch for family and friends, it is the chef's perk to surreptitiously enjoy the first pancake, straight out of the pan, eaten with one's fingers, drenched in sugar and a squirt of lemon.

PREP 10 mins

* plus 30 mins resting

COOK 15 mins

TOTAL 25 mins

DIETARY

USE NON-GLUTEN FLOUR

MAKES

12 x 24CM, SERVES 4

125g plain flour
pinch of salt
1 large egg, plus 1 yolk
250ml semi-skimmed milk
butter, for cooking

TO SERVE
bowl of granulated sugar
zest of 1 lemon and the juice of 2 lemons

Sift the flour and salt into a large mixing bowl. Make a well in the centre, and pour the egg and yolk into it. Mix the milk with 3 tablespoon water and then pour about a quarter of the milk mixture into the flour.

Start whisking the egg and milk together from the centre, gradually drawing the flour into the batter until it is all incorporated and you have a smooth mixture with the consistency of double cream. Whisk in the remaining milk until the batter is more like single cream. Cover and chill in the fridge for at least 30 minutes.

Heat a crêpe pan over a medium–high heat. Add a knob of butter and wipe out any excess using kitchen paper. The batter should sizzle when it hits the pan. Pour a small ladleful of batter into the pan and swirl it around so that the batter spreads out into a thin coat.

Tip any excess batter that doesn't set immediately back into the bowl. When the pancake begins to set and look lacy around the edges, loosen the edges with a spatula and flip it over using the spatula. Alternatively, toss the pancake with swagger. The best way to do this is to loosen the pancake with a spatula, hold the crêpe pan handle with both hands, then jerk the pan upwards and slightly forwards so that the pancake spins, then be sure to move the pan back to catch the pancake. Make sure the pancake is lying flat across the pan with no folds, then cook for 30 seconds or until lightly golden.

I like to serve my pancakes with a bowl of granulated sugar that has lemon zest grated in it and a jug of lemon juice for guests to serve themselves.

Necci

CHESTNUT-FLOUR PANCAKES, WITH SHEEP'S MILK RICOTTA AND CHESTNUT HONEY

An autumnal snack, *necci* is a dish typical of the Tuscan region of the Garfagnana, a mountainous area near Lucca in Italy that is covered in chestnut forests. Traditionally, *necci* are made over an open fire and cooked between a pair of *testi*, cast iron pans that have a long handle rather like a pizza paddle, which are turned to cook both sides of the *necci*. The pans can still be found for sale in Tuscany. Going further back still, *necci* were made by heating up flat terracotta dishes over an open fire. Once hot, they were covered with chestnut leaves before the necci batter was spread on them. Then another layer of chestnut leaves was used to cover the batter, and another stone dish used to cover the mixture. As well as adding to the flavour of the *necci*, the leaves left a leaf imprint on them too. My method is somewhat more straightforward. *Necci* are eaten warm with a dollop of fresh sheep's milk ricotta cheese and a drizzle of chestnut honey. For a special occasion, add some marron glacé for utter chestnut indulgence. For a savoury *necci*, cook some pancetta to serve with the ricotta.

PREP 10 mins

plus resting time

COOK 20 mins

TOTAL 30 mins

DIETARY

CHESTNUT FLOUR IS GLUTEN-FREE

MAKES

12 X 24CM, SERVES 4–6

250g chestnut flour
2 tablespoons extra virgin olive oil, plus extra for cooking
pinch of salt

2 marron glacé (optional), chopped
400g sheep's milk ricotta
chestnut honey, to serve

Preheat the oven to 100°C/gas mark ¼ and warm a plate to keep the pancakes warm while you make them. In a large bowl, mix the flour with enough water to get a smooth, dense batter slightly thicker than a usual crêpe batter; you will need about 300ml water.

Add the olive oil and salt, and mix again. Lightly oil a frying pan over a medium heat.

Add 2 spoonfuls of the batter to the pan and tilt it slightly to coat the pan evenly (note that this batter does not move as fluidly as a crêpe batter). Cook for 2 minutes or until you see that the top of the batter looks dry. Loosen with a spatula, flip over and cook for 1 minute. Keep the pancakes warm and repeat with the remaining batter, adding more oil to the pan as necessary.

When all the *necci* are ready, Add the marron glacé, if using, to the ricotta, then spread some over each *necci*. Fold them in two, or roll them up, and serve them drizzled with chestnut honey.

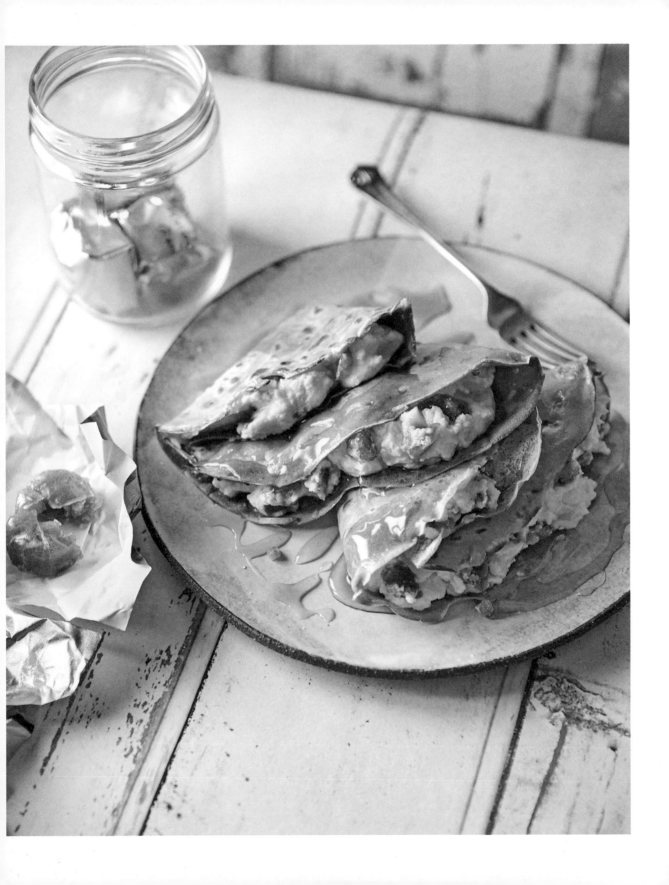

Kaiserschmarrn

An unusual, almost soufflé-like fluffy caramelised pancake, *kaiserschmarrn* is served shredded with plum compote. It is a dessert popular in Austria, southern Germany, Slovenia and northern Croatia. *Kaiserschmarrn* translates colloquially as 'the Emperor's mess' and gets its name from Kaiser Franz Josef I. As ever, there are various apocryphal stories associated with this dish, including one about the ever-so-fussy Empress Elizabeth who was always watching her waistline, so the Kaiser ordered the pancake to be cut up to look less daunting on the plate. I convince myself it is less fattening because it is in little shreds! However, she still decided not to eat it, so the Kaiser, finding it totally moreish, devoured the lot. Another story has the Kaiser on tour and stopping at a farmer's home in the Alps for lunch. The farmer got so flustered that he messed up the pancake and cut it into bits to cover his mistakes and smothered it with plum jam. It is the perfect pancake for a messy cook. The sweet batter with whisked egg whites making it ethereally light is usually made with rum-soaked raisins, although I found it rather better with barberries soaked in port for an unusual and slightly tart contemporary Ottoman twist to the recipe. The pancake is split up with two forks into pieces and finished in butter to make it crisp and completely irresistible. It is traditional to finish the *kaiserschmarrn* with an alpine avalanche of icing sugar on top.

PREP 15 mins

plus 30 mins soaking

COOK 15 mins

TOTAL 30 mins

DIETARY

USE NON-GLUTEN PLAIN FLOUR

MAKES

2 x 24CM, SERVES 4

50g barberries or raisins
2 tablespoons port or dark rum
4 large egg yolks
50g golden caster sugar
pinch of salt
500ml semi-skimmed milk
½ teaspoon vanilla extract
150g plain flour, sifted
5 large egg whites
60g butter
icing sugar, to serve

FOR THE VANILLA AND CINNAMON PLUM COMPOTE
100g soft brown caster sugar
500g plums, pitted and cut into quarters
seeds from 1 vanilla pod
1 cinnamon stick
300g whipping cream
1 teaspoon vanilla extract

Preheat the oven to 100°C/gas mark ¼ and warm a baking tray tray lined with greaseproof paper to keep the pancakes warm while you make them. Put the barberries and port in a bowl to macerate for 30 minutes. Drain and dry on kitchen paper.

Meanwhile, to make the compote, put 200ml of cold water into a large pan over a medium–high heat and add the sugar. Bring to the boil to dissolve the sugar, then let the mixture bubble for 30 seconds.

Add the plums, vanilla seeds and cinnamon stick, and simmer for 8–10 minutes. Transfer the plums to a bowl, and simmer the sauce so that it reduces and thickens. Pour over the plums and leave to cool slightly. Set aside.

Put the whipping cream in a bowl. Add the vanilla extract, then whip with an electric or hand whisk until thick. Set aside.

Put the egg yolks in a bowl and whisk in the sugar and salt until pale yellow and thick. Stir in the milk and vanilla extract, then gradually and gently stir in the flour. Finally, add the barberries.

Just before cooking, put the egg whites into a clean bowl and whisk until they form stiff peaks. Fold into the pancake batter using a metal spoon.

Heat 15g of the butter over a low heat in a deep, heavy frying pan and pour in half the batter to a depth of 5cm. Cook for 3 minutes or until the batter has risen, the top is beginning to set and the underneath is lightly brown. Slide out of the pan and transfer to a plate. Melt a further 15g of the butter around the pan. Using oven gloves, carefully invert the pan over the plate and flip to return the pancake to the pan. Cook the other side for 2–3 minutes until just set.

Using two forks, break the finished pancake into six to eight pieces and put on the preheated baking tray. Keep the pancake warm and repeat with the remaining batter, adding more butter to the pan as before. Break up the second pancake as before.

Heat the remaining butter over a medium heat and cook the pancake pieces for 2 minutes, turning to crisp the ripped edges. Pile them on a plate and drench generously with icing sugar. Serve with the plum compote and whipped vanilla cream.

Layered Crêpe Cake

WITH CHOCOLATE RUM GANACHE AND PRALINE CREAM

Crêpes, chocolate, nuts, rum and cream – this celebration cake really has it all. It's creamy, moist, rich and sophisticated with plenty of interesting texture in each bite. A small slice suffices, although the greedy will ask for seconds. Make the crêpes as thin as you dare. The French might call it a mille-feuille crêpe gateau, although aiming for a 20-layer cake is ambitious enough. The cake definitely improves if kept chilled in the fridge overnight, so it is perfect to make ahead for a special occasion. A great friend who used to be a pastry chef at The Dorchester gave me an insider's insight into how to make praline like a pro.

PREP 60 mins
plus 1 hour resting & chilling

COOK 20 mins

TOTAL 80 mins

DIETARY

USE GLUTEN-FREE PLAIN FLOUR

MAKES

1 24CM CAKE, SERVES 8

350g plain flour
25g good-quality cocoa powder
pinch of salt
2 tablespoons golden caster sugar
900ml semi-skimmed milk
3 tablespoons melted butter, plus extra for cooking
strawberries or cherries in rum or kirsch, to serve

FOR THE PRALINE CREAM
100g golden caster sugar

75g blanched almonds
75g blanched hazelnuts
600ml double cream

FOR THE CHOCOLATE GANACHE
250g good-quality dark chocolate (70% cocoa solids), broken
280ml double cream
3 tablespoons golden caster sugar
50ml espresso
2 tablespoons dark rum

Sift the flour, cocoa powder and salt into a large mixing bowl and stir in the sugar. Gradually whisk in the milk using a hand or electric whisk (the batter should be the consistency of single cream). Add the butter and whisk again. Leave the batter to rest for 30 minutes at room temperature. Pour into a jug.

To make the praline, put the caster sugar into a pan. Add 3 tablespoons water and set the pan over a medium–low heat to allow the sugar to dissolve slowly, stirring. Bring to the boil and continue to cook until the syrup turns a pale amber colour. Working quickly, tip the almonds and hazelnuts into the pan and continue to cook for 1 minute or until the caramel turns a deeper amber and the nuts are a little toasted. Tip the praline onto a baking tray and leave until completely cold and hardened. Break the praline into chunks. Put into a small plastic bag and secure it. Bash with a rolling pin until coarsely chopped. Alternatively, whizz in a food processor. Whip the cream and add the crushed praline. Set aside.

To make the chocolate ganache, melt the chocolate in a heatproof bowl over a pan of gently simmering water, making sure the base of the bowl doesn't touch the water, and stirring occasionally. In a separate small pan, heat the double cream and sugar until it is just abut to boil, turn down the heat, stir in the coffee and rum. Remove from heat. Combine with the chocolate. Cover and cool, then put in the freezer for at least 30 minutes until it thickens.

Warm a heavy non-stick crêpe pan over a medium–high heat. Use a heatproof pastry brush to sparingly cover the pan with melted butter. Use a small cup to pour in equal amounts of batter for each crêpe, using just enough to coat the base of the pan, then swirl it around to spread the batter to the edges. The crêpes should be as thin as possible. Pour any excess batter back into the cup and then into the mixing bowl.

Cook each crêpe for 1 minute or until it is just beginning to go a little crisp at the edges. Flip over and cook for a a further 40–60 seconds. Stack the cooked crêpes on a plate – there is no need to separate them with greaseproof paper. Add a little extra milk if the first crêpes are too thick, and, if the crêpes are not cooking evenly, reduce the heat a little. Repeat with the remaining batter, adding more butter to the pan as necessary. Aim to make about at least 12 crêpes.

Put the first crêpe on a serving plate and spread it with a thin layer of chocolate ganache. Add a second crêpe and spread it with a slightly thicker layer of praline cream. Repeat alternating the layers until all the crêpes and the praline cream and chocolate ganache are used up. Chill the pancake gateau in the fridge for at least 1 hour or preferably overnight before serving.

I serve it with strawberries on the side in summer, or cherries in rum or kirsch would be fabulous for the winter. For added extravagance, an extra jug of single cream on the side could be proffered, although this is probably an indulgence too far!

Walnut and Raisin Palatschinken

WITH CHOCOLATE SAUCE

This decadent dessert crêpe was invented by Károly Gundel of the world-famous grand Budapest Gundel restaurant overlooking the City Park. At Gundel, the pancakes are flambéed with rum at the table, although I prefer to merely add dark rum to the nut filling, which I serve more roughly chopped than the traditional paste, as I find this more flavourful.

PREP

plus 30 mins resting

COOK

TOTAL

DIETARY

USE NON-GLUTEN
PLAIN FLOUR

MAKES

8 X 24CM,
SERVES 4

240g plain flour, sifted
2 tablespoons golden caster sugar
2 large eggs, beaten
1 tablespoon melted butter, plus extra
butter for cooking
350ml semi-skimmed milk

FOR THE FILLING
125g walnuts, toasted in a frying pan
and coarsely chopped
60g raisins
zest of 1 lemon

60g golden caster sugar
4 tablespoons dark rum

FOR THE CHOCOLATE SAUCE
250g plain chocolate, broken into small
pieces
100ml whipping cream
1 large egg yolk
4 tablespoons golden syrup
a knob of butter
pinch of salt

Preheat the oven to 100°C/gas mark ¼ and heat a plate to keep the pancakes warm while you make them. Put the flour in a bowl and stir in the sugar. Add the eggs and melted butter, then gradually incorporate the milk, whisking constantly and taking care to incorporate all the flour. Leave to rest for at least 30 minutes. Transfer to a jug.

Meanwhile, to make the filling, put the walnuts in a bowl and add the raisins, lemon zest, sugar and rum. Mix together, then set aside.

To make the chocolate sauce, put the chocolate and cream in a small heavy-based saucepan over a low heat. Heat, stirring occasionally, until the chocolate has melted into the cream to make a smooth paste. Stir in the egg yolk, followed by the golden syrup, butter and salt to give a glossy sauce. Keep warm over a very low heat.

Heat a frying pan over a medium heat and add a little butter. Spread evenly with kitchen paper removing any excess. Pour in enough batter to cover the pan very sparsely, as *palatschinken* should be ultra-thin. Cook for 1–2 minutes until the underneath is lightly golden and starting to crisp at the edges. Flip over and cook for 1 minute or until lightly golden. Keep the pancakes warm and repeat with the remaining batter to make eight *palatschinken*, adding more butter to the pan as necessary.

To serve, put 1–2 tablespoons of the walnut filling onto each crêpe, roll it up and pour over the warm chocolate sauce.

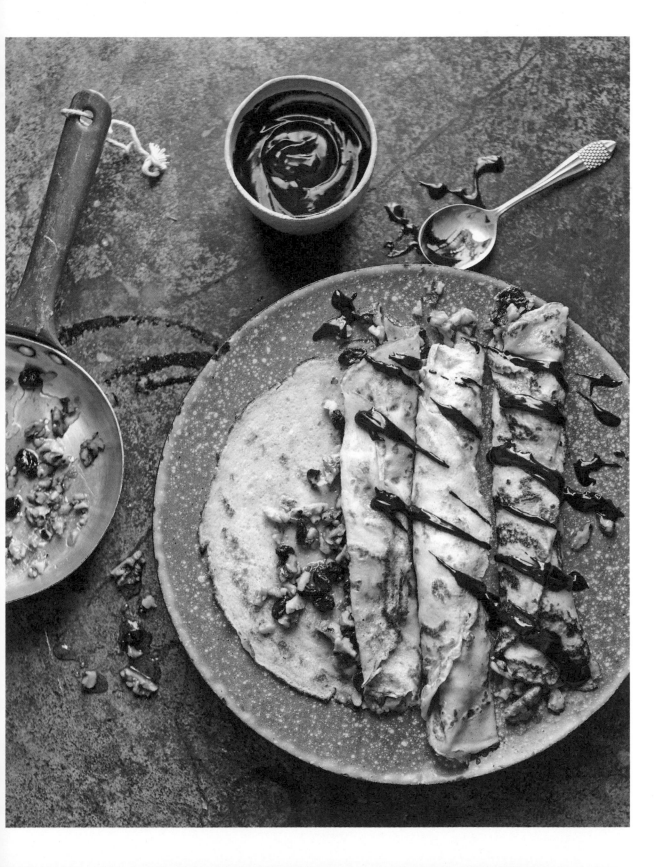

Atayef (Kataif) Arabic Pancake

The gorgeous sweetmeat-like pancake, *atayef*, takes a little practice to get right, but is worth it. The batter needs to be thinner than single cream to perfect the requisite bubbly, filigree-like texture, yet still be able to hold its delectable filling. The *atayef* are cooked for a mere minute to turn pale golden on one side only. The other side is velvety because it is covered with bubbles that allow the flavours of the filling to permeate the atayef.

PREP 20 mins

COOK 20 mins

TOTAL 40 mins

DIETARY

VEGAN

MAKES

*30 x 9CM,
SERVES 6–8*

120g flour
55g semolina
½ teaspoon fast-acting yeast
1 teaspoon baking powder, plus extra
if needed
2 tablespoons golden caster sugar
2 tablespoons groundnut oil
2 tablespoons orange blossom water

FOR THE FILLING
100g almonds, with skins removed
1 teaspoon ground cinnamon
1 teaspoon cardamom seeds, crushed
1 tablespoon light soft brown sugar
1 tablespoon orange blossom water
250g tub clotted cream

Put the flour in a large bowl and add the semolina, yeast, baking powder and sugar, then whisk to mix well. Add the oil, orange blossom water and 375–400ml warm water, whisking until you get a thin well-combined mixture the consistency of single cream. Leave to rest for 30 minutes. Meanwhile, preheat the oven to 200°C/gas mark 6.

To make the filling, put the almonds on a baking tray and roast for 10 minutes. Leave to cool. Put the cooled almonds in a plastic bag, seal and crush with a rolling pin. Pour into a bowl and add the cinnamon, cardamom seeds and sugar. Set aside.

Heat a large non-stick frying pan over a medium heat. Pour 1 tablespoon of the batter to make small atayef. The batter should start to bubble at the sides immediately and spread across the whole surface. If this doesn't happen, the batter is not thin enough, in which case gradually whisk in an additional 50ml warm water and try again. If there are still not enough bubbles, add a further 1 teaspoon baking powder, whisk and have another go. Cook as many pancakes as will fit at one time. Cook for 1 minute – the surface should still be velvety and smooth and lightly golden underneath.

The pancake is only cooked on one side and not flipped. Transfer the *atayef* to a clean tea-towel and fold the tea-towel over to cover and stop the atayef drying out. The *atayef* are stacked bubbly sides together. This is important, as it will soften them making them easier to stuff and seal, and it will prevent them from splitting. Repeat with the remaining batter. (They can be stored stacked bubbly sides together in tightly sealed plastic bags for a few hours, if necessary.)

When the *atayef* are cool, fill them. Stir the orange blossom water into the cream. To fill the *atayef*, fold the *atayef* at one end only and pinch the sides as if making a tiny bouquet. Fill with orange blossom-scented clotted cream and top with the nut mixture.

Pang Jee

THAI COCONUT AND BANANA PANCAKES

I find the combination of coconut and banana irresistible, especially when mixed with the butterscotch richness of palm sugar and the chewy texture of glutinous rice flour. I remember tasting *pang jee* many years ago at a food stall along Lumpini Park in Bangkok. There was a huge queue that I naturally had to join to find out what was so incredibly popular. The *pang jee* were being made at great speed by a very smiley wizened elderly Thai woman in a vivid yellow silk dress. They are delicious served warm as a dessert with vanilla ice cream or as an afternoon snack with jasmine tea.

PREP 15 mins
* plus cooling

COOK 15 mins

TOTAL 30 mins

DIETARY

GLUTEN-FREE

MAKES

18 x 8CM,
SERVES 6

160ml coconut cream
3 tablespoons palm sugar
1 banana or 2 namwa (small ultra-sweet bananas, often available frozen)
60g glutinous rice flour

50g desiccated coconut, unsweetened
50g fresh coconut chunks, if available, finely chopped
pinch of salt

Put the coconut cream in a small pan over a low heat and add the palm sugar. Stir until the sugar has dissolved. Remove from the heat and leave to cool.

In a mixing bowl, mash the banana. Add the rice flour, desiccated coconut, fresh coconut, salt and the coconut-cream mixture. Stir until well combined – it will be a very thick batter.

Heat a non-stick frying pan over a medium–low heat. No oil is required. Drop tablespoonfuls of batter onto the pan into a round shape about 3cm wide. Cook as many pancakes as will fit at one time. Cook for 1–2 minutes until the base is golden. Flip over and press down slightly, then cook for a further 1–2 minutes or until golden. Cool slightly on a wire rack.

Pang jee are best served warm, but they are delicious at room temperature too.

Baked Caramelised Apple Pancake

This traditional German pancake made with caramelised apple slices flavoured with cinnamon then topped with a sweet batter reminds me of a tarte tatin's gorgeous indulgence. I like to add a little calvados or kirsch to the batter to amp it up. As it's cooked in a very hot oven, the eggy batter bubbles and puffs up dramatically, so serve it at once to enjoy the full impact. Nutmeg ice cream or the brown-sugar whipped cream used here complements it beautifully. Confusingly, these pancakes are usually referred to as 'Dutch babies' in the US and Canada. They've recently become an Instagram obsession. The name was supposedly coined in the early 1900s by the daughter of the owner of Manca's Café, a family-run restaurant in Seattle, Washington. The café no longer exists, yet the name lives on. The 'Dutch' refers to the group of German–American immigrants known as the Pennsylvania Dutch, although 'Dutch' is understood to be a corruption of Deutsch. Savoury Dutch babies filled with goat's cheese and parmesan, rosemary and thyme are great too.

PREP 10 mins

COOK 20 mins

TOTAL 30 mins

DIETARY

USE GLUTEN-FREE
PLAIN FLOUR

MAKES

1 x 24CM,
SERVES 4

50g butter

4 large eating apples (Braeburn are good), peeled, cored and sliced

4 tablespoons light soft brown sugar, plus 30g extra

1 teaspoon ground cinnamon

125g plain flour, sifted

3 tablespoons golden caster sugar

¼ teaspoon salt

175ml semi-skimmed milk

50ml Greek yogurt

3 large eggs, beaten

1 teaspoon vanilla extract

2 tablespoon calvados or kirsch (optional)

300ml whipping cream

Preheat the oven to 230°C/gas mark 8.

Melt the butter in a large 24cm ovenproof, non-stick frying pan over a medium heat. Add the sliced apples and sprinkle over the 4 tablespoons brown sugar and the cinnamon.Cook the apples gently for 8–10 minutes until just starting to soften and caramelise, then transfer the apple to a plate. Set aside.

Meanwhile, in a large bowl, mix the flour, sugar and salt. In a separate bowl, whisk the milk, yogurt, eggs, vanilla and calvados, if using. Add to the flour mixture and whisk again to ensure there are no lumps and the batter has the consistency of double cream.

Pour the batter over the apples. Put into the hot oven and cook for 15–20 minutes until the batter has puffed up, has just started to set in the centre and is turning golden at the edges. While it is cooking, put the whipping cream and 30g brown sugar in a bowl and whip with an electric or hand whisk until the sugar is gently incorporated. Transfer the cream to a serving bowl. When the apple pancake is cooked, immediately turn it out of the pan and serve it cut into wedges with the brown-sugar whipped cream.

Dorayaki

JAPANESE HONEY PANCAKES WITH AZUKI BEAN AND MASCARPONE FILLING

Legend has it that *dorayaki* were first prepared when a samurai named Benkei accidently left his gong (dora) behind at a farmer's house where he was hiding out. The enterprising farmer used it to cook little 'gong cakes', hence the name. Manga comic books have made *dorayaki* extremely popular among children in Japan, especially served sandwiched with Nutella and accompanied by a glass of milk.

PREP 15 mins

COOK 15 mins
* plus cooling

TOTAL 30 mins

DIETARY

USE GLUTEN-FREE
PLAIN FLOUR

MAKES

8 x 9CM SANDWICHES,
SERVES 4

1 large egg, beaten
1 large egg, separated
1 tablespoon golden caster sugar, plus
3 teaspoons
1 tablespoon clear honey
½ teaspoon vanilla extract
1 tablespoon sunflower or rapeseed oil,
plus extra for cooking

75ml semi-skimmed milk
80g flour, sifted
1 teaspoon baking powder

FOR THE FILLING
100g adzuki red bean mixture
200g mascarpone

Put the beaten egg and egg yolk in large bowl. Add 1 tablespoon sugar, the honey, vanilla, oil, milk, flour and baking powder. Mix gently with a whisk, starting from the middle of the bowl and moving outwards until all the ingredients are just incorporated and the mixture is foamy and falls in ribbons when the whisk is lifted from the bowl.

Put the egg white in a clean bowl with the remaining sugar and, using an electric whisk, slowly whisk until it forms soft peaks, then increase the speed to form stiff peaks. Add about a third of the egg white to the egg-yolk mixture using a hand whisk and a very light circular motion. Repeat with the second third of egg white. Now use a spatula to fold in the remaining egg white, ensuring that the mixture remains full of air bubbles and doesn't deflate. If it does, the dorayaki will be flat and rubbery.

Heat a crêpe pan over a medium heat, add 1 tablespoon oil, then wipe off any excess with kitchen paper. The pan should be sufficiently oiled for the dorayaki to cook to an enticing pale golden colour, but not so much that they colour unevenly. Add 1 generous tablespoon of batter for each dorayaki, and swirl it around quickly to a diameter of about 8cm. Cook for 1–2 minutes until golden. Check it is done by tentatively sliding a spatula underneath. If there are no wet crumbs sticking to the spatula, it is ready to flip over. Cook for 40–60 seconds until golden yet still a little soft in the centre. Transfer to a wire rack to cool completely. Repeat with the remaining batter, adding more oil to the pan as before.

When the *dorayaki* are cool, put the adzuki mixture in a bowl, add the mascarpone and combine well. Use 1 heaped tablespoonful to sandwich two similar-sized *dorayaki* together, spreading the filling with a palette knife. If the *dorayaki* are not to be eaten straightaway, wrap them in clingfilm to stop them drying out. They can also be frozen for up to 1 month.

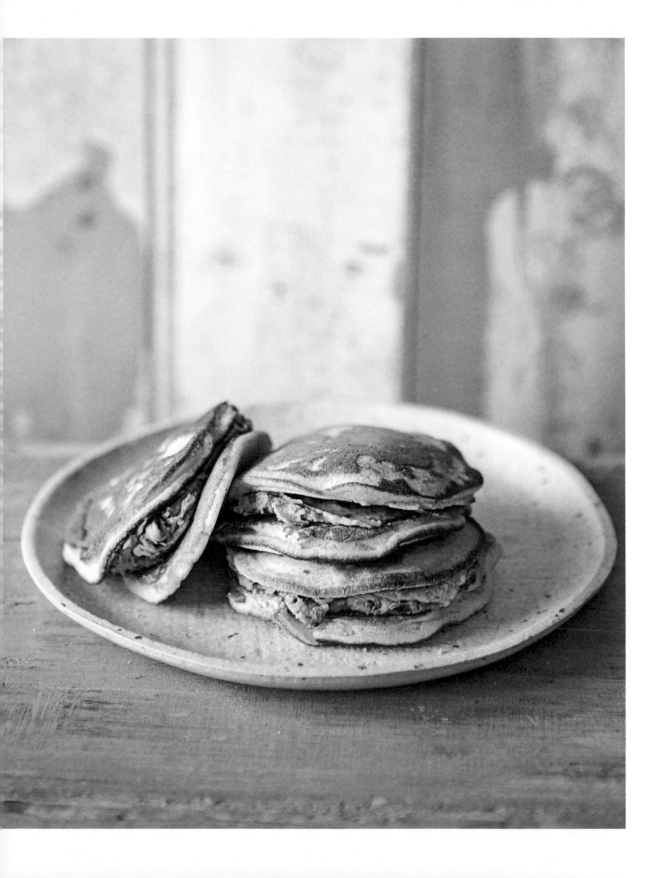

Index

Acknowledgements

There are so many people I want to thank, I barely know where to start.

An enormous thank you to Kyle Cathie for recognising the need for a new book dedicated to pancakes around the world that I've long wanted to write. I greatly enjoyed working with such a calm, organised and consultative team whose company has been a huge pleasure, especially Judith Hannam, Sophie Allen, Hannah Coughlin, Victoria Scales and Julia Barder.

Thank you so much to my agent Martine Carter for all her cajoling, encouragement and patience.

I am in photographic awe of the astonishingly talented Maja Smend, who has made sure that every pancake looks exquisite and different. Equally, I've been hugely impressed by Lizzie Harris for not only her speedy and ever delicious culinary skills in cooking up my recipes, but her great sense of style, enthusiasm and fun in ensuring every dish is gorgeous and inspiring. Rosie Mackean, too, for being such an eagle-eyed, quick and knowledgeable assistant with impeccable Spanish. Thanks to Tonia Shuttleworth for finding so many beautiful and interesting props. I coveted so many of those plates.

I hugely appreciate all the encouragement, love and help so many friends have given me with bringing the book together and, especially Jo Lamiri for her endless enthusiasm and sharing so much indispensable critical feedback and laughter, especially on late night aebelskiver and wine sessions. Louise Simpson for masses of support, particularly on blintzes making and taking over her kitchen. Helen Mangham, one of my oldest and best friends, whom I once shared a kitchen with in those heady post-university days, for indulging my pancake making and research over a wonderful, fun stay at her home in SW France. Huge, huge thanks to Philip Owens of Bespoke Menu Design, a dear friend and enormous creative culinary influence on me. Helen Hokin for being so excited about the book and her indispensable feedback and creative marketing insight. Vivienne Huang and Loretta Liu for their generous input on some of my Asian recipes. Romy Gill, for kindly helping me with an easy dosa recipe. Food writers, including Jill Norman, Diana Henry, Jenny Linford, Catherine Phipps and Sabrina Ghayour for their much appreciated advice and insight. Mary Craig for her intelligent and incisive critical input. My wonderful neighbour Serena Rowe for so much enthusiasm, fun and being a great taster for impromptu supper parties. Deep thanks to Francis Pigott, with whom I discovered Hampstead's creperie kiosk long ago and our gorgeous, memorable holiday in Brittany involving so many galettes. My big-hearted, generous parents for giving me such a strong food background and for embracing so many tastings, remembering pancakes past and giving so much love and support. I promise I will make you atayif again!

Thanks to Sous Chef, a brilliant resource for the more recondite ingredients, Billington's and Shipton Mill for their great products, Lakeland, Greenpan and Borough Kitchen for indispensable kitchen equipment.

And finally, not least, to my son Theo for always been enthusiastic and giving creative feedback when it was pancakes yet again for supper.